Great Passenger Ships of the World

Volume 3: 1924–1935

Roma

Great Passenger Ships of the World

Volume 3: 1924–1935

Arnold Kludas

Translated by Charles Hodges

PSL

Patrick Stephens, Cambridge

First published in Germany under the
title
Die Grossen Passagierschiffe der Welt
First published in Great Britain—1976

ISBN 0 85059 245 3

Text filmset in 10 on 12 pt English 49 by
Stevenage Printing Limited, Stevenage.
Printed on 100 gsm Fineblade cartridge
and bound by The Garden City Press
Limited, Letchworth, Herts.
Published by Patrick Stephens
Limited, Bar Hill, Cambridge,
CB3 8EL, England.

Foreword

This third volume continues the documentation up to the year 1935. This section includes a highly interesting period—the second half of the '20s. This was when great and famous ships were introduced on to all routes, and the period comes to its climax in the new prestige contest for the Blue Riband, which was gained by the Bremen *in 1929, and subsequently went to the superliners* Normandie *and* Queen Mary.

The large number of friendly letters I received following the publication of the first two volumes in Germany, in addition to favourable reviews in the Press, have served to give me great satisfaction and have also encouraged me in the often very tedious detailed research. I do hope that this volume will meet with the same reception as its predecessors. I should also like to thank all those who have helped me in the preparation of this volume, particularly Hans Graf from Hamburg, Rudi Kleyn from Voorburg, Dr H.H. Kuhlmann from Munich, J.F. van Puyvelde and the late Paul E.R. Scarceriaux from Brussels and Dr G. Spazzapan from Savona.

Arnold Kludas

Hamburg: January, 1976.

Explanatory Notes

All passenger ships ever launched having a gross registered tonnage (GRT) of over 10,000 are presented in the five volumes of this work. This third volume deals with the period 1924 to 1935. The ships are arranged chronologically, with the exception of sister-ships or groups of ships which have been placed together regardless of exact chronology. The chronological order of the individual sections has been determined from the launching date of the first ship of the class or group. The technical/historical biography of each ship appears under the name with which the ship first entered service. This applies also if the ship sailed later under other names and for other shipping companies. This rule is departed from only in exceptional circumstances. To trace a particular ship the reader is recommended to use the Index of Ships' Names, pages 239/240. In cases where ships have been renamed these are included after the first name in each case, as a further help in tracing all the later names, each with the year of the name change. The following is a guide to the technical and historical information concerning the ships.

I. Technical Data

The information given in the paragraph on technical data applies fundamentally to the date when the ship first went into service as a passenger carrier. Planned specifications are given in the case of incompleted ships for which at their respective stages of construction these had not been fully decided upon. Alterations affecting technical data are noted with historical notes against the appropriate dates.

Dimensions Length overall × moulded breadth in metres rounded off to one place of decimals, followed by the equivalent in feet, the length to the nearest whole number and breadth to one place of decimals. Length overall has been adopted in preference to other length measurements. It was found that recorded registered length and length between perpendiculars could vary from time to time and from place to place.

Propulsion Type of machinery, constructor. Where the shipbuilder has not been responsible for the propelling machinery, its constructor is given. The abbreviations III or IV exp eng indicate triple or quadruple expansion (steam) engines.

Power The figure of horse power given is the highest performance attainable by the engines in normal service. The different methods of measuring horse power, according to the form of propulsion, are as follows:
IHP = indicated horse power, unit of measurement for reciprocating steam engines and internal combustion engines.
SHP = shaft horse power, unit of measurement for turbine machinery and internal combustion engines.
BHP = brake horse power, unit of measurement for internal combustion engines.
The horse power figures, thus arrived at through different methods, cannot necessarily be compared with each other. While BHP and SHP are practically identical, their relationship to the indicated horse power (IHP) is in the region of 4:5. 8,000 SHP is thus equivalent to 10,000 IHP.

Speed Service speed is given in knots. This is followed, as far as can be established, by the highest speed achieved on trials with the engines running at maximum power.

Passengers On nearly all ships the passenger accommodation and the number of berths for each class were frequently altered. Even if it were still possible today to establish all these changes exactly, the necessary effort would not justify the value of the figures thus obtained. One can come to completely different conclusions however correct the figures, for sofa-berths or emergency beds may or may not have been included. The information on alterations to passenger accommodation therefore is limited to really significant modifications, as far as it has been possible to determine them. The standard in the lowest-priced classes of passenger accommodation varied from ship to ship, and between owners and routes, from large mass dormitories (which could be used alternatively for the carriage of cargo) to relatively comfortably equipped rooms with a moderate number of beds. On many ships these variations existed side by side under the general description of 'third class'.

Crew Crew-strength also was subject to alteration, as for instance when a ship was converted from coal to oil-firing, or when the passenger capacity was changed. Changes in crew-strength have not been noted. Unfortunately it has not been possible to determine crew strength for every ship.

II Historical Data

The historical information reflects in chronological order the career of the ship, giving all important events and facts.

Owners In the ships' biographies, shipowners are indicated throughout by what are considered to be the accepted short-forms in English-speaking countries. Nevertheless, a selected short-form may not itself be based on an English translation of a non-English title, for instance: Nippon Yusen KK, CGT, etc. It is assumed that Cie, Cia, AG, SA, etc, will be as familiar to readers as are such English abbreviations as SN, Co, Corp, etc. After the name of a shipowner, the location mentioned in each case is the ship's home port, which is not necessarily where the shipowner has his head office. An alphabetical list of all shipowners with their complete styles is included as an appendix to Volume 5.

Builders Like shipowners, builders are noted throughout by their accepted

Contents

short-forms, and are listed alphabetically with their complete styles in Volume 5.

Completion Completion-date is the date of commencement of trials.

Routes Ports of call are omitted from the information concerning routes.

Newly-built Ships for Messageries Maritimes

Steamship *Champollion*
Messageries Maritimes, Marseille

Builders: Constructions Navales,
La Ciotat
Yard no: 149
12,263 GRT; 158.5 × 19.1 m /
520 × 62.7 ft; III exp eng from
builders; Twin screw; 10,000 IHP;
15 max 16.5 kn; Passengers: 188
1st class, 133 2nd class, 128 3rd
class, 500 steerage; Crew: 310.

1924 Mar 16: Launched.
1925 Completed.
After one Mediterranean cruise the
Champollion began her maiden
voyage in the Marseille-Alexandria
service on September 14.
1933 Nov: Rebuilding commenced
at La Ciotat which lasted until
1934. New, longer, Maierform
forepart. Additional low pressure
turbines fitted. Now 14,000 IHP;
17.5, max 19 knots. Length overall
167.6 m /550 ft. 12,644 GRT.
1940 Laid up at Algiers.
1942 Dec: Taken over as troop
transport by the Allies.
1946 Returned to owners. Used in
passenger and troop transport
service Marseille-Far East.
1950 Sep: Refitted and
modernised at La Ciotat. Only one
funnel. Passenger
accommodation: 207 1st class, 142
2nd class, 150 3rd class. 12,546
GRT.
1951 Mar: On completion of refit,
re-entered Marseille-Alexandria
service.
1952 Dec 22: In the early morning
the *Champollion* was approaching
Beirut in bad weather. After she
had sighted the Ras-Beirut
lighthouse course was set for entry.
Shortly afterwards the ship was
stranded on the Elchat Elmalhoun

reef, two nautical miles south of
the harbour entrance. It was later
established that the ship's
navigators had set course based on
a beacon of the then still to be
opened Khaedé airport, which
happened to be working that
morning and had the same
frequency as the Ras Beirut
lighthouse.
Although the *Champollion* was
only lying 200 yards from the
beach, the situation for those on
board was extremely serious. The
lifeboats could not be used because
of the heavy seas. In the meantime
the ship had developed a
considerable list and broke apart
abaft the funnel. Not until the
evening of December 22 were a few
people rescued. The bad weather
continued the next day and the
Champollion appeared about to
capsize. Eventually Beirut pilots
were able to approach the wreck
and in several trips rescued in their
boats everyone still on board. 15
people had died in the rescue
attempts of the previous day.
The wreck was sold for scrap to a
Lebanese firm.

1-3 *The three rebuilding stages of the*
Champollion. (*1*) *First form up to*
1933. (*2*) *Second form 1934-1950.* (*3*)
The Champollion's *appearance from*
1951.

1

2

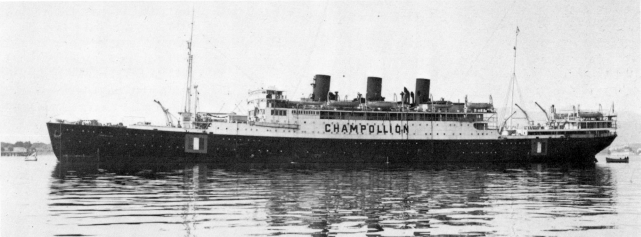

3

Steamship *Mariette Pacha*
Messageries Maritimes, Marseille

Builders: Constructions Navales,
La Ciotat
Yard no: 150
12,239 GRT; 158.5 × 19.1 m /
520 × 62.7 ft; III exp eng from
builders; Twin screw; 10,000 IHP;
15, max 16 kn; Passengers: 188
1st class, 133 2nd class, 128 3rd
class, 500 steerage; Crew: 310.

1925 Feb 8: Launched.
Completed.
Marseille-Alexandria service.
1940 Laid up at Marseille.
1944 Aug: Sunk by German
troops in the evacuation of
Marseille. Raised and broken up
after the war.

Steamship *D'Artagnan*
Messageries Maritimes, Marseille

1942 *Teiko Maru*

Builders: Ch et A de la Gironde,
Bordeaux
Yard no: 181
15,105 GRT; 172.3 × 19.8 m /
565 × 65.0 ft; III exp eng from
builders; Twin screw; 10,800 IHP;
15, max 16.5 kn; Passengers: 165
1st class, 155 2nd class, 100 3rd
class; Crew: 350.

1924 Apr 23: Launched.
1925 Completed.
Aug 28: Maiden voyage Marseille-
Far East.
1941 Oct: Burned out at
Shanghai.
1942 Seized and repaired by the
Japanese. Placed in service as
transport *Teiko Maru*.
1944 Feb 22: The *Teiko Maru* was
torpedoed and sunk by the US
submarine *Puffer* off the Natuna
Islands in the Pacific.

Turbine steamer *Athos II*
Messageries Maritimes, Marseille

Builders: AG 'Weser', Bremen
Yard no: 392
15,275 GRT; 172.5 × 20.1 m /
566 × 66.0 ft; Geared turbines,
'Weser'; Twin screw; 9,500 SHP;
15, max 16 kn; Passengers: 165 1st
class, 155 2nd class, 100 3rd class;
Crew: 350.

1925 Nov 12: Launched.
1927 Jan: Completed.
Mar 25: Maiden voyage
Marseille-Far East.
1937/38 Machinery refit at La
Ciotat. Two additional turbines
fitted. Now 16,000 SHP. 16.5, max
18.5 knots. Passengers: 84 1st
class, 108 2nd class, 112 3rd class.
1938 May 27: First voyage after
refit.
1940 Laid up at Algiers.
1942 Dec: Taken over as troop
transport by the Allies.
1946 Far East service again for
Messageries Maritimes.
1959 Aug 3: Arrived at La Spezia
to be broken up.

4

4 *The* Champollion's *sister ship,*
Mariette Pacha.
5/6 *The* D'Artagnan *and* Athos II,
built for the Far East service.

5

6

Steamship *Explorateur Grandidier*
Messageries Maritimes, Marseille

Builders: Penhoët, St Nazaire
Yard no: C5
10,268 GRT; 145.0 × 18.5 m /
476 × 60.7 ft; III exp eng;
Penhoët; Twin screw; 6,800 IHP;
14 kn; Passengers: 141 1st class, 90
2nd class, 68 3rd class.

1924 Nov 26: Launched.
1925 Dec 1: Completed.
Marseille-Madagascar service.
1940 Laid up at Marseille.
1944 Aug: Sunk by German
troops in the evacuation of
Marseille in order to block
harbour. Broken up after the war.

Turbine steamer *Bernardin de
Saint Pierre*
Messageries Maritimes, Marseille

1942 *Teibi Maru*

Builders: Tecklenborg,
Wesermünde
Yard no: 399
10,268 GRT; 145.0 × 18.5 m /
476 × 60.7 ft; Geared turbines,
Tecklenborg; Twin screw; 6,000
SHP; 14 kn; Passengers: 141 1st
class, 90 2nd class, 68 3rd class.

1925 Sep 3: Launched.
1926 Sep: Completed.
Nov 11: Maiden voyage
Marseille-Madagascar.
1942 Jun: Seized by the Japanese

at Saigon. Renamed *Teibi Maru*.
1943 Oct 10: The *Teibi Maru* was
torpedoed off Annam by the US
submarine *Bonefish* and sank in
position 14°49′ N-110°16′ E.

7

7-9 *The sister-ships* Explorateur Grandidier (*7*) *and* Bernardin de Saint Pierre (*8/9*) *were built for the Marseille-Madagascar service.*

The Five 20,000 tonners of the Orient Line

Turbine steamer *Orama*
Orient Line, Barrow

Builders: Vickers, Barrow
Yard no: 598
19,777 GRT; 200.6 × 22.9 m /
659 × 75.1 ft; Geared turbines
from builders; Twin screw; 20,000
SHP; 20 kn; Passengers: 592 1st
class, 1,244 3rd class.

1924 May 20: Launched.
Originally intended name was
Oriana.
Oct 25: Completed.
Nov 15: Maiden voyage
London-Brisbane.
1935 19,819 GRT.
1938 19,840 GRT.
1940 Troop transport.
Jun 8: While serving in the British
evacuation of Norway the *Orama*
was intercepted in the North Sea
by the German heavy cruiser
Admiral Hipper and sunk by
gunfire. Fortunately there were no
troops on board the *Orama*. 280
members of the crew were rescued
by the Germans.

Turbine steamer *Oronsay*
Orient Line, Glasgow

Builders: Brown, Clydebank
Yard no: 500
20,001 GRT; 200.6 × 22.9 m /
659 × 75.1 ft; Geared turbines,
Brown; Twin screw; 20,000 SHP;
20 kn; Passengers: 590 1st class,
1,250 3rd class.

1924 Aug 14: Launched.
1925 Jan 14: Completed.
Feb 7: Maiden voyage London-
Brisbane.
1938 20,043 GRT.
1939 Troop transport.
1942 Oct 9: The *Oronsay* was
sunk by four torpedoes from the
Italian submarine *Archimede* off
West Africa in position 04°29′ N–
20°52′ W. Five dead.

1

1/2 *The* Orama (*1*) *was sunk in 1940*
by the German cruiser Admiral
Hipper.
3 *The* Oronsay *was sunk in 1942.*

2

3

Turbine steamer *Otranto*
Orient Line, Barrow

Builders: Vickers, Barrow
Yard no: 619
20,032 GRT; 200.6 × 22.9 m /
659 × 75.1 ft; Geared turbines,
Vickers; Twin screw; 20,000 SHP;
20 kn; Passengers: 572 1st class,
1,114 3rd class.

1925 Jun 9: Launched.
Dec: Completed.
1926 Jan 9: Maiden voyage
London-Brisbane.
1935 3rd class passenger
accommodation became tourist
class.
1939 Troop transport.
1948/49 Refitted at Liverpool for
return to civilian service. 20,051
GRT. 1,412 tourist class
passengers.
1949 Jul 14: First post-war voyage
London-Sydney.
1957 Jun: Sold to be broken up at
Faslane.
Aug: Arrived at Faslane for
scrapping by British Iron & Steel
Corp.

Turbine steamer *Orford*
Orient Line, Barrow

Builders: Vickers, Barrow
Yard no: 627
19,941 GRT; 200.5 × 22.9 m /
658 × 75.1 ft; Geared turbines,
Vickers; Twin screw; 20,000 SHP;
20 kn; Passengers: 550 1st class,
1,150 3rd class.

1927 Sep 29: Launched.
1928 Sep: Completed.
Oct 13: Maiden voyage London-
Brisbane.
1938 20,043 GRT.
1939 Troop transport.
1940 Jun 1: The *Orford* was
bombed by German aircraft off
Marseille and set on fire. She was
beached and subsequently
completely burned out.
1947 The wreck was salvaged and
scrapped at Savona.

Turbine steamer *Orontes*
Orient Line, Barrow

Builders: Vickers Armstrong,
Barrow
Yard no: 637
19,970 GRT; 202.3 × 22.9 m /
664 × 75.0 ft; Geared turbines
from builders; Twin screw; 20,000
SHP; 20 kn; Passengers: 500 1st
class, 1,112 3rd class.

1929 Feb 26: Launched.
Jul: Completed.
After a few cruises she started her
maiden voyage London-Brisbane
on October 26.
1938 20,097 GRT.
1940 Troop transport until 1947.
1947 Refitted and overhauled by
Thornycroft, Southampton.
20,186 GRT.
502 1st class, 610 tourist class.
1948 Jun 17: First post-war voyage
London-Sydney.
1953 One-class ship for 1,410
tourist class passengers.
1962 Sold to Ordaz & Co,
Valencia, to be broken up.
Mar 5: Arrived at Valencia.

4 *Orient Liner* Otranto.
5 *The* Orford *proved to be another
victim of the war.*
6 *The* Orontes *sailed in Orient Line's
Australia service until 1962.*

4

5

6

Motorship Aorangi

Motorship *Aorangi*
Union SS Co of New Zealand,
London

Builders: Fairfield, Glasgow
Yard no: 603
17,491 GRT; 182.9 × 22.0 m /
600 × 72.2 ft; Sulzer diesel,
Fairfield; Quadruple screw; 13,000
BHP; 17.5, max 18.24 kn;
Passengers: 436 1st class, 284 2nd
class, 227 3rd class; Crew: 328.

1924 Jun 17: Launched.
Dec 16: Completed.
1925 Jan 2: Maiden voyage
Southampton-Vancouver.
Feb 6: First voyage Vancouver-
Sydney.
1931 Aug: Transferred to the
Canadian Australasian Line,
London, a company formed by
Canadian Pacific and the Union
SS Co for the Vancouver-Sydney
service.
1938 Passenger accommodation
altered: 248 1st class, 266 cabin
class, 125 3rd class.
1940 Feb 10: Troop transport.
1944 Jul: Accommodation and
depot-ship, from 1945 in Pacific
ports.
1946 Apr: Released from naval
service.
Passenger ship again. 212 1st
class, 170 cabin class, 104 3rd
class.
1948 Aug 19: First post-war
voyage Sydney-Vancouver.
1953 Jun 9: Sold to the British
Iron & Steel Corp to be broken up.
Jul 25: Arrived at Dalmuir. Broken
up by Arnott Young & Co.

1 *The* Aorangi *was launched in June
1924, the first large passenger
motorship. Shown here with a white
hull which only appeared in 1948/49.
Afterwards repainted green.*

1

Motorship *Monte Sarmiento*
Hamburg-South America Line,
Hamburg

Builders: Blohm & Voss,
Hamburg
Yard no: 407
13,625 GRT; 159.7 × 20.1 m /
524 × 66.0 ft; MAN geared diesel,
B & V; Twin screw; 6,800 BHP;
14, max 14.5 kn; Passengers:
1,328 3rd class, 1,142 steerage;
Crew: 280.

1924 Jul 31: Launched.
Nov 12: Completed.
Nov 15: Maiden voyage Hamburg-
La Plata ports.
Cruising.
1939 Dec 21: Accommodation
ship for the German Navy at Kiel.
1942 Feb 26: The *Monte
Sarmiento* was sunk in an Allied
air raid on Kiel.
1943 The wreck raised, towed to
Hamburg and scrapped.

1 *When she entered service the* Monte
Sarmiento *was for a few weeks the
largest motorship in the world.*

1

Motorship *Monte Olivia*
Hamburg-South America Line,
Hamburg

Builders: Blohm & Voss,
Hamburg
Yard no: 409
13,750 GRT; 159.7 × 20.1 m /
524 × 66.0 ft; MAN geared diesel,
B & V; Twin screw; 6,800 BHP;
14, max 14.5 kn; Passengers: 1,372
3rd class, 1,156 steerage; Crew:
280.

1924 Oct 28: Launched.
1925 Apr 4: Completed.
Apr 23: Maiden voyage Hamburg-
La Plata ports.
Cruising.
1939 Oct 19: Arrived at Hamburg
from Santos after breaking
through the blockade.
1940 Jan 4: Naval accommodation
ship.
1945 Feb 15: Hospital ship.
Transported wounded from the
German eastern territories to Kiel.
Apr 3: The *Monte Olivia* bombed
and sunk at Kiel.
1946 Jun: Scrapping commenced
which lasted until 1948.

Motorship *Monte Cervantes*
Hamburg-South America Line,
Hamburg

Builders: Blohm & Voss,
Hamburg
Yard no: 478
13,913 GRT; 159.7 × 20.1 m /
524 × 66.0 ft; MAN geared diesel,
B & V; 6,800 BHP; Twin screw;
14, max 14.5 kn; Passengers:
1,354 tourist class, 1,138 steerage;
Crew: 280.

1927 Aug 25: Launched.
1928 Jan 3: Completed.
Jan 7: Maiden voyage Hamburg-
La Plata ports.
Cruising.
Jul 25: During a cruise in Arctic
waters the ship was damaged by ice
and began to take in water. She
made for Spitzbergen and the
Soviet icebreaker *Krassin* was
asked to assist. The leaks were
repaired by July 30.
1930 Jan 22: During a voyage
around Tierra del Fuego the
Monte Cervantes ran onto hitherto
uncharted submerged rocks, was
holed, and began to sink. The

1,117 passengers were ordered into
the boats. The ship slipped from
the rocks, and in an attempt to
beach her she was driven onto the
Eclaireur Reef, where she
remained fast. On the following
day the passengers' baggage was
taken off.
Jan 24: There were only a few of
the crew on board when the ship
suddenly capsized. All were
rescued except her master who lost
his life.
1951 The Italian salvage company
Savamar began work on the wreck,
the stern of which was still
protruding from the water.
1954 Jul: The ship was
successfully raised.
Oct 14: In the course of an attempt
to tow the temporarily patched
wreck to Ushuaia, the *Monte
Cervantes* finally sank in deep
water.

2

2/3 *The* Monte Olivia *at the Hamburg Overseas Landing Stage, and* (*3*) *outward bound on the Elbe.*
4 *The unfortunate* Monte Cervantes.

Motorship *Monte Pascoal*
Hamburg-South America Line,
Hamburg

Builders: Blohm & Voss,
Hamburg
Yard no: 491
13,870 GRT; 159.7 × 20.1 m /
524 × 66.0 ft; MAN geared diesel,
B & V; Twin screw; 6,800 BHP;
14, max 14.5 kn; Passengers:
1,372 tourist class, 1,036 steerage;
Crew: 280.

1930 Sep 17: Launched.
1931 Jan 15: Completed.
Jan 26: Maiden voyage Hamburg-
La Plata ports.
Cruising.
1939 Oct 14: Arrived at Hamburg
from Buenos Aires after breaking
through the blockade.
1940 Jan 11: Accommodation ship
for the Navy yard at
Wilhelmshaven.
1944 Feb 3: Completely burned
out and sank during bombing of
Wilhelmshaven.
May 12: Raised after sealing and
pumping-out.
1945 May: British war prize.
1946 Dec 31: Loaded with
chemical warfare munitions, the
Monte Pascoal was sunk by the
British at Skagerrak.

5/6 *The* Monte Pascoal *in 1936 (5) and
as a naval accommodation ship (6).*

Motorship *Monte Rosa*
Hamburg-South America Line,
Hamburg

1946 Empire Windrush

Builders: Blohm & Voss,
Hamburg
Yard no: 492
13,882 GRT; 159.7 × 20.1 m /
524 × 66.0 ft; MAN geared diesel,
B & V; Twin screw; 6,800 BHP;
14, max 14.5 kn; Passengers:
1,372 tourist class, 1,036 steerage;
Crew: 272.

1930 Dec 4: Launched.
1931 Mar 21: Completed.
Maiden voyage Hamburg-La
Plata ports.
Cruising.
1940 Jan 11: Naval
accommodation ship at Stettin.
1942 Troop transport Denmark-
Norway.
1943 Oct: Until March 1944,
served as workshop for repairs to
the battleship *Tirpitz*.
1944 Troop transport again. After
striking a mine, was refitted as
hospital ship.
1945 Feb 16: Off Hela the *Monte
Rosa* struck a mine and was
damaged aft. Listing and with a
flooded engine room the ship was
towed to Gotenhafen (Gydnia).
She was temporarily repaired with
materials available on board, and
then towed to Copenhagen
carrying over 5,000 refugees and
wounded.
May: Taken to Kiel.
Nov 18: British war prize.
Repaired and fitted out as troop
transport at South Shields.
14,414 GRT.
1946 Renamed *Empire Windrush*.
Managed for the Ministry of
Transport by the New Zealand
Line, London.
1950 14,651 GRT after refit.
1954 Mar 28: During a voyage
from Yokohama to England the
Empire Windrush caught fire in
the Mediterranean near Cape
Caxine after an explosion in the
engine room. Four dead. The
passengers and crew abandoned
ship and were picked up by other
vessels. The British destroyer
Saintes tried to tow the burning
ship to Gibraltar.
Mar 29: The *Empire Windrush*
sank.

7 *The* Monte Rosa *in Hamburg
harbour in 1931.*
8/9 *A wartime picture of the troop
transport* Monte Rosa *and a
photograph of the ship as a British war
prize on the Tyne, shortly before she
was renamed* Empire Windrush.

7

8

9

The Statendam

Turbine steamer *Statendam*
Holland-America Line, Rotterdam

Builders: Harland & Wolff,
Belfast
Yard no: 612
29,511 GRT; 212.5 × 24.8 m /
697 × 81.4 ft; Geared turbines,
H & W; Twin screw; 22,000 SHP;
19, max 20 kn; Passengers: 510 1st
class, 344 2nd class, 374 tourist
class, 426 3rd class.

1921 Laid down. Many hold-ups
in building before launching.
1924 Sep 11: Launched. Further
work temporarily halted due to US
immigration restrictions.
1927 Apr 13: Towed to Schiedam
for completion. Work continued at
Wilton's.
1929 Mar 16: Completed.
Apr 11: Maiden voyage
Rotterdam-New York.
1933 28,291 GRT.
1939 Dec: Laid up at Rotterdam.
1940 May 11: In the fighting
around Rotterdam the *Statendam*
was hit by German bombs and
caught fire. By May 14 the ship
had been completely burned out.
Aug: The wreck was towed to
Hendrik Ido Ambacht and
scrapped.

1 *An impressive picture of the*
Statendam, *which entered service in*
1929.
2 *The burnt-out wreck of the*
Statendam *in May 1940.*

1

2

Steamship *Razmak*
P & O Line, Greenock

1930 Monowai

Builders: Harland & Wolff, Greenock
Yard no: 659
10,602 GRT; 158.2 × 19.0 m / 519 × 62.3 ft; IV exp eng; H & W; Twin screw; 12,000 IHP; 18 kn; Passengers: 142 1st class, 142 2nd class.

1924 Oct 16: Launched.
1925 Feb 26: Completed.
Mar 13: Maiden voyage London-Aden.
Entered service on Aden-Bombay route.
1926 Marseille-Bombay service.
1928 10,852 GRT.
1929 P & O Line withdrew their Marseille-Aden-Bombay service.
1930 Sold to Union SS Co of New Zealand. Renamed *Monowai*.
Nov 27: First voyage Sydney-San Francisco. Accommodation for 483 passengers in two classes.

Additional low pressure turbines fitted. Speed now 19, max 20 knots.
1933 Sydney-Vancouver service in the Canadian Australasian Line's timetable. Home port now Wellington.
1934 Used on Wellington-Sydney service.
1935 Several more voyages Sydney-Vancouver.
1936 Laid up until 1939.
1940 Aug 30: Armed merchant cruiser in the Royal New Zealand Navy.
1943 Jun: Troop transport.
1946 Aug: Released from naval service.
1949 Jan: After overhaul and refit at Sydney, re-entered Wellington-Sydney service. Now 11,037 GRT. Passengers: 181 1st class, 205 tourist class.
1960 Sep 6: The *Monowai* arrived at Hong Kong, where she was broken up.

Steamship *Ranpura*
P & O Line, Newcastle

Builders: Hawthorn, Leslie & Co, Newcastle
Yard no: 532
16,585 GRT; 173.7 × 21.7 m / 570 × 71.2 ft; IV exp eng from builders; Twin screw; 15,000 IHP; 17 kn; Passengers: 310 1st class, 280 2nd class; Crew: 380.

1924 Sep 13: Launched.
1925 Mar 23: Completed.
Apr 3: Maiden voyage London-Bombay.
1926 16,601 GRT. From 1933, 16,688 GRT.
1939 Dec: In service as Royal Navy armed merchant cruiser.
1942 Sold to the British Admiralty, which had her converted to a repair ship. The work lasted until 1944.
1961 Sold to be broken up at La Spezia.

1

2

3

1/2 *The P & O express steamer*
Razmak *was sold to New Zealand in*
1930. (2) The ship as the Monowai
after the 1949 refit.
3 *The* Ranpura *as a Royal Navy repair*
ship.

Steamship *Ranchi*
P & O Line, Newcastle

Builders: Hawthorn, Leslie & Co,
Newcastle
Yard no: 534
16,650 GRT; 173.7 × 21.7 m /
570 × 71.2 ft; IV exp eng from
builders; Twin screw; 15,000 IHP;
17 kn; Passengers: 308 1st class,
282 2nd class; Crew: 380.

1925 Jan 24: Launched.
Jul 28: Completed.
Aug: Maiden voyage London-
Bombay.
1931 16,738 GRT. Additional low
pressure turbines fitted.
1939 Oct 23: Fitted out at Bombay
as armed merchant cruiser.
Second funnel removed.
1943 Mar: The *Ranchi* became a
troop transport.
1947 Jul: Refit as one-class
emigrant ship commenced by
Harland & Wolff, which lasted
until 1948. 16,974 GRT.
1948 Jun 17: First voyage London-
Sydney.
1953 Jan: Sold to be broken up at
Newport, Mon.

Steamship *Rawalpindi*
P & O Line, Greenock

Builders: Harland & Wolff,
Belfast
Yard no: 660
16,619 GRT; 173.2 × 21.7 m /
568 × 71.2 ft; IV exp eng, H & W;
Twin screw; 15,000 IHP; 17 kn;
Passengers: 310 1st class, 290 2nd
class; Crew 380.

1925 Mar 26: Launched.
Sep 3: Completed.
Entered London-Bombay-Far East
service.
1931 16,697 GRT.
1939 Sep: Armed merchant
cruiser. Second funnel removed.
Nov 23: While patrolling between
Iceland and the Faroes the
Rawalpindi was intercepted by the
German battleships *Gneisenau*
and *Scharnhorst*. After a short
exchange of fire the hopelessly
outgunned armed merchant
cruiser was drifting with the wind,
burning and out of action. The
German battleships saved 26
British seamen, but then broke off
the rescue action as British forces

were sighted. Three hours later the
Rawalpindi sank. 270 of her
complement had died.

4/5 The Ranchi *in the '30s (4) and
about the year 1950 (5).*
6 The famous Rawalpindi *during
trials. In 1939, while serving as an
armed merchant cruiser, she was sunk
by two German battleships.*

4

5

6

Steamship *Rajputana*
P & O Line, Greenock

Builders: Harland & Wolff,
Greenock
Yard no: 661
16,568 GRT; 173.2 × 21.7 m /
568 × 71.2 ft; IV exp eng, H &
W; Twin screw; 15,000 IHP; 17
kn; Passengers: 307 1st class, 288
2nd class; Crew: 380.

1925 Aug 6: Launched.
Dec 30: Completed.
1926 Jan: Maiden voyage London-
Bombay.
1933 16,644 GRT.
1939 Sep: Armed merchant
cruiser. Second funnel removed.
1941 Apr 13: The *Rajaputana* was
sunk by two torpedoes from the
German submarine *U 108* west of
Ireland in position 64°50′ N-
27°25′ W. 41 dead.

Steamship *Cathay*
P & O Line, Glasgow

Builders: Barclay, Curle & Co,
Glasgow
Yard no: 602
15,104 GRT; 166.1 × 21.4 m /
545 × 70.2 ft; IV exp eng from
builders; Twin screw; 13,000 IHP;
16, max 17.5 kn; Passengers: 203
1st class, 103 2nd class.

1924 Oct 31: Launched.
1925 Mar: Completed.
Mar 27: Maiden voyage London-
Sydney.
1927 15,121 GRT. 1932 measured
at 15,272 GRT and 1934, 15,225
GRT.
1939 Oct 11: Armed merchant
cruiser.
1942 Troop transport.
Nov 11: During the Allied landing
in North Africa the *Cathay* was

bombed by German aircraft off
Bougie, and sank on the following
day. One dead.

7/8 *The* Rajaputana *in London (7) and
off Colombo (8).*
9 *The* Cathay, *the first of three sister-
ships for the Australia service.*

7

Steamship *Comorin*
P & O Line, Glasgow

Builders: Barclay, Curle & Co, Glasgow
Yard no: 603
15,116 GRT; 166.1 × 21.4 m / 545 × 70.2 ft; IV exp eng from builders; Twin screw; 13,000 IHP; 16, max 17.5 kn; Passengers: 203 1st class, 103 2nd class.

1924 Oct 31: Launched.
1925 Apr 11: Completed.
Apr 25: Maiden voyage London-Sydney.
1927 15,132 GRT.
1930 Additional low pressure turbines fitted. 15,279 GRT. From 1934, 15,241 GRT.
1939 Sep: Armed merchant cruiser.
1941 Apr 6: The *Comorin* caught fire in mid-Atlantic, and had to be abandoned. The crew was rescued by the British destroyers *Lincoln* and *Brooke,* and other warships.

Steamship *Chitral*
P & O Line, Glasgow

Builders: Stephen, Glasgow
Yard no: 504
15,248 GRT; 167.0 × 21.4 m / 548 × 70.2 ft; IV exp eng, Stephen; Twin screw; 13,000 IHP; 16 kn; Passengers: 199 1st class, 135 2nd class.

1925 Jan 27: Launched.
Jun 12: Completed.
Jul 3: Maiden voyage London-Sydney.
1930 Additional low pressure turbines fitted. 17 knots. 15,396 GRT.
1935 15,346 GRT.
1939 Oct: Armed merchant cruiser.
1944 April until September: fitted out as troop transport at Baltimore.
1947 Sep: Refit commenced at London as one-class emigrant ship, lasting until 1948. 15,555 GRT.
1948 Dec 30: First voyage London-Sydney.
1953 Apr: Sold to be broken up at Dalmuir.

Turbo-electric vessel *Viceroy of India*
P & O Line, Glasgow

Builders: Stephen, Glasgow
Yard no: 519
19,648 GRT; 186.5 × 23.2 m / 612 × 76.1 ft; Turbines from Stephen, electric driving motors from British Thomson-Houston Co; Twin screw; 17,000 SHP; 19 kn; Passengers: 415 1st class; 258 2nd class; Crew: 420.

1928 Sep 15: Launched.
Originally to have been named *Taj Mahal.*
1929 Feb 19: Completed.
Entered London-Bombay service.
1934 19,627 GRT.
1942 Nov 11: Serving as troop transport during the Allied landing in North Africa, the *Viceroy of India* disembarked her troops at Algiers and sailed for England. However, she was torpedoed and sunk by the German submarine *U 407* 34 nautical miles off Oran, in position 36°26′ N-00°24′ W. Four dead. The survivors were picked up by the British destroyer *Boadicea.*

10

11

12

10 *The* Comorin *during trials.*
11/12 *The troopship* Chitral *(11) and the same ship in 1950 as an emigrant carrier.*
13 *The* Viceroy of India, *the first large turbo-electric passenger ship.*

13

Gripsholm and Kungsholm

Motorship *Gripsholm*
Swedish-America Line,
Gothenburg

1955 *Berlin*

Builders: Armstrong, Whitworth
& Co, Newcastle
Yard no: 999
17,993 GRT; 174.6 × 22.7 m /
573 × 74.5 ft; Burmeister & Wain
diesel; Twin screw; 13,500 BHP;
16, max 17 kn; Passengers: 127 1st
class, 482 2nd class, 948 3rd class;
Crew: 360.

1924 Nov 26: Launched.
1925 Nov 7: Delivered.
Nov 21: Maiden voyage
Gothenburg-New York.
1927 Measurement: 17,716 GRT.
From 1937, 18,134 GRT.
1940/46 Almost continuously in
the service of the International Red
Cross, exchanging prisoners and
wounded.
1946 Mar: First post-war voyage
as passenger ship New York-
Gothenburg.
1949 Rebuilding commenced at
Howaldt Kiel, lasting until the
spring of 1950. Forepart
lengthened, new funnels,
passenger accommodation
modernised. Length overall
179.8 m/590 ft. 19,105 GRT.
Passengers: 210 1st class, 710
tourist class.
1952 Jul 18: The *Gripsholm*
rescued 45 of the crew of the
burning Norwegian cargo vessel
Black Hawk 75 nautical miles from
New York.
1954 Feb 1: First voyage
Bremerhaven-New York for the
Bremen-America Line, Bremen,
which was founded on a 50% each
participation basis by North
German Lloyd and the Swedish-
America Line.
1955 Jan 7: North German Lloyd
took over the *Gripsholm*, and
renamed her *Berlin*. Passenger
accommodation: 98 1st class, 878
tourist class. 18,600 GRT.
1966 Nov 26: Arrived at La
Spezia, where she was broken up
by Terrestre Marittima.

1/2 *The* Gripsholm *in the '20s (1) and
after the 1937 refit (2).*
3 *The* Gripsholm's *appearance in the
'50s.*
4 *The* Berlin *ex* Gripsholm.

1

2

3

4

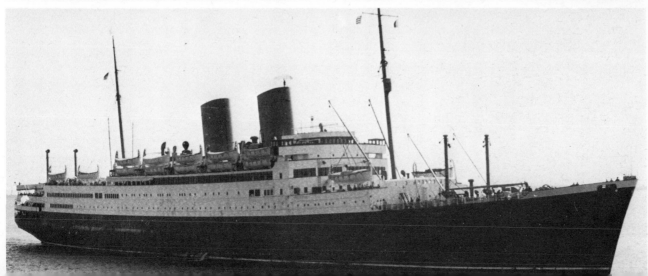

Motorship *Kungsholm*
Swedish-America Line,
Gothenburg

1942 *John Ericsson*
1948 *Italia*
1964 *Imperial Bahama*

Builders: Blohm & Voss,
Hamburg
Yard no: 477
20,223 GRT; 185.6 × 23.8 m /
609 × 78.1 ft; Burmeister & Wain
diesel; Twin screw; 17,000 BHP;
17.5 max 18.5 kn; Passengers: 115
1st class, 490 2nd class, 970 3rd
class; Crew: 340.

1928 Mar 17: Launched.
Oct 13: Completed.
Oct 14: Three men killed by an
explosion in the engine room
during trials.
Nov 24: Maiden voyage
Gothenburg-New York.

1932/33 Passenger
accommodation reconstructed.
1935 19,955 GRT.
1937 20,067 GRT.
1939 Cruising from New York
after outbreak of war.
1942 Jan 2: Sold to the US War
Shipping Administration.
Renamed *John Ericsson*.
Troop transport, managed by
United States Lines.
1947 Mar: Badly damaged by fire
at New York.
Jul: Bought back by
Swedish-America Line.
Dec: Sold to Home Lines (South
Atlantic Lines), Panama. Repaired
and refitted by Ansaldo, Genoa.
21,554 GRT.
1948 Apr 8: Renamed *Italia*.
Jul 27: First voyage Genoa-South
America.
1949 Jun 12: First voyage Genoa-
New York.
1950 Panama measurement:

16,777 GRT.
1952 Mar: First voyage Hamburg-
New York. Managed by Hamburg-
America Line. Passengers: 213 1st
class, 1,106 tourist class.
1954 Oct 6: During a docking
manoeuvre at Steubenhöft,
Cuxhaven, the tug *Fairplay 1* got
caught under the *Italia's* bow and
was forced underwater. Two dead.
1958 Refit of passenger
accommodation commenced by
Howaldt Hamburg, lasting until
spring 1959. 140 1st class, 1,150
tourist class.
1959 Mar 24: First voyage
Hamburg-Quebec.
1961 New York-Nassau service
and cruising.
1964 Sold to Freeport Bahama
Enterprises. Renamed *Imperial
Bahama,* and used as floating
hotel.
1965 Sep 8: Arrived at Bilbao to
be broken up.

5

5 *The* Kungsholm *of the Swedish-America Line.*
6/7 *During the Second World War the* Kungsholm *sailed under the American flag as the* John Ericsson (*6*) *not returning to passenger service until 1948, as the* Italia (*7*).

Motorship *Pieter Corneliszoon Hooft*
Stoomv Mij 'Nederland', Amsterdam

Builders: A et Ch de la Loire, St. Nazaire
Yard no: 256
14,642 GRT; 164.6 × 20.7 m / 540 × 67.9 ft; Sulzer diesel; Twin screw; 10,500 BHP; 15, max 16 kn; Passengers: 205 1st class, 273 2nd class, 107 3rd class, 54 4th class; Crew: 300.

1925 Jan 24: Launched.
Nov: The planned delivery date had to be postponed until January 1926, because of a shipyard strike.
Dec 20: The passenger accommodation on the almost completed ship was totally destroyed by fire.
1926 Jul 21: The builders were not able to keep to the date set for the commencement of trials. The owners transferred the ship to Amsterdam, where the large amount of remaining work was carried out.
Aug 27: Trials and delivery.
The *Pieter Corneliszoon Hooft* was placed in the Amsterdam-Dutch East Indies service.
1931 Rebuilt by Rotterdamsche DD Mij. Forepart lengthened. New Sulzer diesels fitted. 14,729 GRT. 14,000 BHP, 17.5 knots. Length overall 167.3 m / 549 ft.
Apr: First voyage after rebuilding.
1932 Nov 14: The *Pieter Corneliszoon Hooft* was completely destroyed by fire at Amsterdam.
Dec: The wreck was towed to Hendrik Ido Ambacht to be scrapped.

Motorship *Christiaan Huygens*
Stoomv Mij 'Nederland', Amsterdam

Builders: Nederlandsche Sb Mij, Amsterdam
Yard no: 186
15,637 GRT; 173.7 × 20.9 m / 570 × 68.6 ft; Sulzer diesel; Twin screw; 11,600 BHP; 16.5, max 17 kn; Passengers: 269 1st class, 250 2nd class, 53 3rd class; Crew: 290.

1927 Sep 28: Launched.
1928 Jan 25: Completed.
Placed in Amsterdam-Batavia service.
1931 15,704 GRT. 1937, 16,286 GRT.
1940 Troop transport. Managed by Orient Line.
1945 Aug 26: During a voyage Antwerp-Rotterdam the *Christiaan Huygens* struck a mine near Westkapelle and had to be beached, badly damaged, on Zuid Steenbank. One dead. On September 5 the ship broke in two.

1

1/2 *Motorship* Pieter Corneliszoon
Hooft *in 1929. In November 1932 the
ship was totally destroyed by fire at
Amsterdam* (*2*).
3 *Nederland liner* Christiaan Huygens.

Transylvania and Caledonia

Turbine steamer *Transylvania*
Anchor Line, Glasgow

Builders: Fairfield, Glasgow
Yard no: 595
16,923 GRT; 168.3 × 21.4 m /
552 × 70.2 ft: Geared turbines,
Fairfield; Twin screw; 13,500
SHP; 16, max 17 kn; Passengers:
279 1st class, 344 2nd class, 800
3rd class.

1925 Mar 11: Launched.
Sep 2: Completed.
Sep 12: Maiden voyage Glasgow-
New York.
1939 Sep: Armed merchant
cruiser.
1940 Aug 10: The *Transylvania*
was torpedoed by the German
submarine *U 56* off Malin Head in
position 55°50′ N-08°03′ W. She
was taken in tow but sank before
reaching the coast. 48 dead.

Turbine steamer *Caledonia*
Anchor Line, Glasgow

1939 *Scotstoun*

Builders: Stephen, Glasgow
Yard no: 495
17,046 GRT; 168.3 × 21.4 m /
552 × 70.2 ft; Geared turbines,
Stephen; Twin screw: 13,500 SHP;
16, max 17 kn; Passengers: 205 1st
class, 403 2nd class, 800 3rd class.

1925 Apr 21: Launched.
Sep 25: Completed.
Oct 3: Maiden voyage Glasgow-
New York.
1939 Sep: Armed merchant
cruiser. Renamed *Scotstoun*.
1940 Jun 13: The *Scotstoun* was
torpedoed and sunk by the
German submarine *U 25* 200
nautical miles west of Inishtrahull
in position 57°00′ N-09°57′ W.
Six dead.

1/2 *The three-funnelled* Transylvania
(*1*) *and* Caledonia (*2*) *sailed in the
Anchor Line's Glasgow-New York
service.*

The Berlin

Steamship *Berlin*
North German Lloyd, Bremen

1949 *Admiral Nachimow*

Builders: Bremer Vulkan,
Vegesack
Yard no: 614
15,286 GRT; 174.3 × 21.1 m /
572 × 69.2 ft; III exp eng,
Vulkan; Twin screw; 12,000 IHP;
16 kn; Passengers: 220 1st class,
284 2nd class, 618 3rd class; Crew:
326.

1925 Mar 24: Launched.
Sep 17: Completed.
Sep 26: Maiden voyage
Bremerhaven-New York.
1928 Nov 13: The *Berlin* rescued
23 survivors from the British
passenger steamer *Vestris,* which
had sunk in a storm the previous
day.
1929 Passenger accommodation:
257 cabin class, 261 tourist class,
361 3rd class.
1938 Oct: Laid up at
Bremerhaven.
1939 May: Two cruises for 'Kraft
durch Freude' ('Strength through
Joy').
Jul 17: Boiler explosion off
Swinemünde, where the ship was
to have been taken over by the
German Navy. 17 dead.
The *Berlin* was repaired at
Hamburg and fitted out as naval
hospital ship.
1944 Accommodation ship.

1945 Feb 1: The *Berlin* sank after
hitting a mine off Swinemünde.
1949 Raised by the Soviets.
Renamed *Admiral Nachimow*.
Repaired and refitted at the
Warnow yard, Warnemünde.
1957 May: Delivered to Soviet
state shipping line. Home port
Odessa. 17,053 GRT. Placed in
service in the Black Sea on the
Odessa-Batum route.

1

2

3

1/2 *The* Berlin *leaving the builders in
1925 (1) and as a hospital ship during
the Second World War (2).*
3 *In 1957 the Soviet state shipping line
placed the* Admiral Nachimow *ex*
Berlin *into service.*

Lloyd Sabaudo and Cosulich Liners

Turbine steamer
Conte Biancamano
Lloyd Sabaudo, Genoa

1942 *Hermitage*
1947 *Conte Biancamano*

Builders: Beardmore, Glasgow
Yard no: 640
24,416 GRT; 198.9 × 23.2 m /
653 × 76.1 ft; Geared turbines,
Beardmore; Twin screw; 24,000
SHP; 20, max 21 kn; Passengers:
280 1st class, 420 2nd class, 390
3rd class, 660 4th class; Crew: 500.

1925 Apr 23: Launched.
Nov 2: Completed.
Nov 20: Maiden voyage Genoa-
New York.
1932 Jan: To 'Italia' Flotta
Riunite, Genoa. Genoa-La Plata
service.
1935 A few voyages as troop
transport to Massawa.
1937 To Lloyd Triestino.
Apr 16: One voyage Trieste-
Shanghai, then refitted in Genoa.
Passengers: 230 1st class, 481 2nd
class, 704 3rd class. 23,255 GRT.
Aug 24: First voyage Genoa-
Shanghai.
1939 Chartered to 'Italia' SAN for
Genoa-Buenos Aires service.
1940 Jan 21: The *Conte
Biancamano* took part in the
rescue action of the Italian
passenger ship *Orazio*, which was
on fire in the Mediterranean. Laid
up at Colón after Italy entered the
war.
1941 Dec: Seized by the US
authorities at Balboa.
1942 Aug 14: Became US Navy
transport *Hermitage* (AP 54).
1946 Aug 20: Released from the
Navy.
1947 Aug 14: Returned to the

Italian Government. Name once
more *Conte Biancamano*. Passed
from the State owned 'Finmare' to
management by 'Italia' SAN.
23,562 GRT after refit and
lengthening. Length overall
202.7 m/665 ft. Passengers: 215
1st class, 333 cabin class, 1,030
tourist class.
1949 Nov 10: First post-war
voyage Genoa-La Plata. Usually in
Genoa-New York service during
the summer months.
1960 Apr 21: Laid up at Naples.
Aug 16: Arrived at La Spezia.
Broken up by Terrestre Marittima.

1/2 The Conte Biancamano *as a Lloyd
Sabaudo liner (1) and as an 'Italia'
ship after her refit in 1949.*

Turbine steamer *Conte Grande*
Lloyd Sabaudo, Genoa

1942 *Monticello*
1947 *Conte Grande*

Builders: Stabilimento Tecnico,
Trieste
Yard no: 764
25,661 GRT; 199.6 × 23.2 m /
655 × 76.1 ft; Geared turbines
from builders; Twin screw; 26,000
SHP; 20, max 21.8 kn; Passengers:
578 1st class, 420 2nd class, 720
3rd class; Crew: 532.

1927 Jun 29: Launched.
1928 Feb: Completed.
Apr 3: Maiden voyage Genoa-New
York.
1932 Jan: To 'Italia' Flotta
Riunite, Genoa.
1933 Genoa-La Plata service.
1935 A few voyages Trieste-New
York during the Abyssinian War.
1940 Laid up at Santos after Italy
entered the war.
1941 Aug 22: Seized by the
Brazilian government.
1942 Apr 16: Sold to the US
Government. Fitting out as troop
transport commenced, which
lasted until September.
US Navy transport *Monticello* (AP
61). 23,861 GRT.
1946 Mar 22: Released from the
Navy.
1947 Jul: Returned to Italy.
Passed from 'Finmare' to
management by 'Italia' SAN.
Renamed *Conte Grande*. 23,842
GRT after refit and lengthening.
Length overall 203.3 m /667 ft.
Passengers: 215 1st class, 333
cabin class, 950 tourist class.
1949 Jul 14: First post-war voyage
Genoa-Buenos Aires. Used for
Genoa-New York service in the
summer months until 1956.
1960 One voyage to Sydney for
Lloyd Triestino.
1961 Sep 7: Arrived at La Spezia
to be broken up.

3/4 *The* Conte Grande *in 1933 (3) and
in 1950 (4).*

3

4

Motorship *Saturnia*
Cosulich Soc Triestina di Nav,
Trieste

1945 *Frances Y. Slanger*
1946 *Saturnia*

Builders: Cant Nav Triestino,
Monfalcone
Yard no: 160
23,940 GRT; 192.5 × 24.3 m /
632 × 79.7 ft; Burmeister & Wain
diesel from builders; Twin screw;
20,000 SHP; 19, max 21 kn;
Passengers: 279 1st class, 257 2nd
class, 309 3rd class, 1,352 4th
class; Crew: 441.

1925 Dec 29: Launched.
1927 Sep 18: Completed.
Sep 21: Maiden voyage Trieste-
La Plata ports.
1928 Feb 1: First voyage Trieste-
New York.
1932 Jan: The Cosulich Line
formally became a member of
'Italia', but retained considerable
independence until it was absorbed
in 'Italia' SAN in January 1937.
1935 May 8: Troop transport to
East Africa.
Dec 24: To Monfalcone for refit.
New Sulzer diesel. 28,000 SHP, 21
knots. 24,470 GRT.
1936 Aug: Back in service.
1940 Jun: Laid up at Trieste.
1942 Mar: Chartered to the
International Red Cross for
evacuation voyages from East
Africa. Afterwards laid up at
Trieste.
1943 Sep 8: Made for an Allied
port following the Italian capitulation.
Taken over by the US Navy as
troop transport.
1945 Jan: Refit commenced as
hospital ship *Frances Y. Slanger,*
lasting until June.
Nov: Released from service as
hospital ship.
1946 US Army transport from
February until June.
Renamed *Saturnia.*
Dec 1: Back to 'Italia' SAN.
1947 Jan 20: First post-war voyage
Genoa-New York. Passenger
accommodation: 240 1st class, 270
cabin class, 860 tourist class.
1950 24,346 GRT.
1955 Nov 8: Trieste-New York
service.
1965 Apr 10: Laid up at Trieste.
Oct 7: Arrived at La Spezia to be
broken up.
1966 Apr: Scrapping commenced
by Terrestre Maritima.

5/6 Cosulich liner Saturnia *in her early
service years (5) and with 'Italia' in the
'50s (6).*

Motorship *Vulcania*
Cosulich Soc Triestina di Nav,
Trieste

1966 *Caribia*

Builders: Cant Nav Triestino,
Monfalcone
Yard no: 161
23,970 GRT; 192.5 × 24.3 m /
632 × 79.7 ft; Burmeister & Wain
diesel from builders; 20,000 SHP;
19, max 21 kn; Passengers: 279 1st
class, 257 2nd class, 310 3rd class,
1,350 4th class; Crew: 440.

1926 Dec 18: Launched. Laid
down as *Urania*.
1928 Dec 1: Completed.
Dec 19: Maiden voyage
Trieste-New York.
1932 Jan: In a similar way to the
Saturnia, the *Vulcania* formally
joined 'Italia', but was not
integrated into 'Italia' SAN until
January 1937.
1935 Feb 2: Troop transport to
East Africa.
May 12: To Monfalcone for refit.
New FIAT diesel. 28,000 SHP, 21,
max 23.3 knots. 24,469 GRT.
Dec 21: Following the refit, back
in Trieste-New York service.
1941 Troop transport voyage
Taranto to Tripoli. Afterwards laid
up at Trieste.
1942 Mar: Chartered to the
International Red Cross for
evacuation voyages from East
Africa. Afterwards laid up at
Trieste.
1943 Sep 8: Sailed following the
Italian capitulation. The *Vulcania*
took on board in Pola cadets from
the Italian Naval Academy and
made for an Allied port by way of
Venice.
Oct: US Army transport.
1946 Dec 14: Back to 'Italia' SAN.
1947 Jul: First post-war voyage
Genoa-South America.
Sep 4: First post-war voyage
Genoa-New York. 24,496 GRT.

Passengers: 240 1st class, 270
cabin class, 860 tourist class.
1955 Oct 28: Trieste-New York
service.
1965 Sold to Sicula Oceanica,
Palermo. Renamed *Caribia*.
1966 Feb: Re-entered service after
refit of passenger accommodation:
337 1st class, 368 cabin class and
732 tourist class.
Southampton-West Indies service
and cruising.
1972 Sep 23: During the night of
September 24 the *Caribia* ran onto
submerged rocks off Nice. The
engine room flooded and was put
out of action.
Sep 29: Laid up at La Spezia.
1973 Sep 18: Arrived at Barcelona
to be broken up.
1974 Resold to Taiwan.
Mar 15: The *Caribia* left
Barcelona in tow for Kaohsiung.

7

7/8 *The Cosulich motorship* Vulcania
(7) joined 'Italia' like her sister-ship
Saturnia. *Picture 8 shows the ship in
the '50s.*
9 *The* Caribia *ex* Vulcania.

Steamship *Llandovery Castle*
Union-Castle Line, London

Builders: Barclay, Curle & Co,
Glasgow
Yard no: 606
10,609 GRT; 148.4 × 18.8 m /
487 × 61.7 ft; IV exp eng from
builders; Twin screw; 6,000 IHP;
13.5, max 14.5 kn; Passengers:
221 1st class, 186 3rd class.

1925 Jul 4: Launched.
Sep 25: Completed.
London-round Africa service.
1941 Mar: Hospital ship.
1946 Sep: Returned to owners.
1947 May: First post-war voyage
London-round Africa.
1953 Sold to British Iron & Steel
Corp to be broken up.

Steamship *Llandaff Castle*
Union-Castle Line, London

Builders: Workman, Clark & Co,
Belfast
Yard no: 488
10,786 GRT; 149.3 × 18.8 m /
490 × 61.7 ft; IV exp eng from
builders; Twin screw; 6,000 IHP;
13.5, max 14.5 kn; Passengers:
224 1st class, 186 3rd class.

1926 Aug 10: Launched.
Nov 24: Completed.
1927 Jan 6: Maiden voyage
London-round Africa.
1940 Troop transport.
1942 Nov 30: The *Llandaff Castle*
was torpedoed and sunk by the
German submarine *U 177* 100
nautical miles south-east of
Lourenço Marques in position
27°20′ S-33°40′ E. Three dead.

Motorship *Llangibby Castle*
Union-Castle Line, London

Builders: Harland & Wolff, Govan
Yard no: 841 G
11,951 GRT; 154.5 × 20.2 m /
507 × 66.3 ft; Burmeister & Wain
diesel, H & W; Twin screw; 8,600
BHP; 14.5 kn; Passengers: 250 1st
class, 200 3rd class.

1929 Jul 4: Launched.
Nov 21: Completed.
Dec 5: Maiden voyage London-
round Africa.
1939 Troop transport.
1942 Jan 16: In the Atlantic the
Llangibby Castle was struck by a
torpedo from the *U 402* and lost
her stern and rudder. However,
she was able to reach Horta under
her own power.
1946 Dec: Returned to owners.
1947 Jul: London-round Africa
service again after refit. 12,039
GRT.
1954 Jul: Sold to be broken up.

1/2 The steamships Llandovery Castle
(1) and Llandaff Castle *entered service
in 1925/26.*
3 The Llangibby Castle *entered
service in 1929.*

2

3

Motorship *Dunbar Castle*
Union-Castle Line, London

Builders: Harland & Wolff, Govan
Yard no: 851 G
10,002 GRT; 147.5 × 18.6 m /
484 × 61.0 ft; Burmeister & Wain
diesel, H & W; Twin screw; 6,300
BHP; 14.5, max 15.9 kn;
Passengers: 200 1st class, 260 3rd
class.

1929 Oct 31: Launched.
1930 May 20: Completed.
London-round Africa service.
1940 Jan 9: On a voyage London-
Beira in convoy the *Dunbar Castle*
struck a mine two nautical miles
northeast of North Goodwins and
sank within 30 minutes. Nine
dead.

Motorship *Carnarvon Castle*
Union-Castle Line, London

Builders: Harland & Wolff,
Belfast
Yard no: 595
20,063 GRT; 199.9 × 22.7 m /
656 × 74.5 ft; Burmeister & Wain
diesel, H & W; Twin screw; 15,000
BHP; 16, max 18.4 kn;
Passengers: 311 1st class, 276 2nd
class, 266 3rd class; Crew: 350.

1926 Jan 14: Launched.
Jun 1: Completed.
Jul 16: Maiden voyage
Southampton-Cape Town.
1937/38 Rebuilt by Harland &
Wolff. New Burmeister & Wain
diesels, forepart lengthened, only
one funnel. 20,123 GRT;
209.2 m /686 ft length overall;
26,000 BHP; 20 knots; passengers:
226 1st class, 245 2nd class, 188
tourist class.
1938 Jul 8: First voyage after
rebuilding, Southampton-Cape
Town.
1939 Sep 8: Entered service as
armed merchant cruiser at

Simonstown.
1940 Dec 5: Action in the South
Atlantic with the German auxiliary
cruiser *Thor*. After 70 minutes the
Carnarvon Castle turned away on
fire, and made for Montevideo.
Four dead.
1944 Fitted out as troop transport
at New York.
1947 Mar: Released from war
service. Refitted as one-class
emigrant ship for 1,283 passengers
in the Southampton-Cape Town
service.
1949/50 Overhauled and rebuilt
at Harland & Wolff. 20,141 GRT.
passengers: 216 1st class, 401
tourist class.
1950 Jun 15: Southampton-Cape
Town service again.
1962 Sep 8: Arrived at Mihara,
Japan, to be broken up.

4

4 *The* Dunbar Castle *was lost in 1940
through striking a mine.*
5 *The* Carnarvon Castle *around 1935.*
6 *The* Carnarvon Castle *entering
Montevideo after her battle with the*
Thor *in December 1940.*
7 *After the war the* Carnarvon Castle
sailed as a one-class ship until 1949.

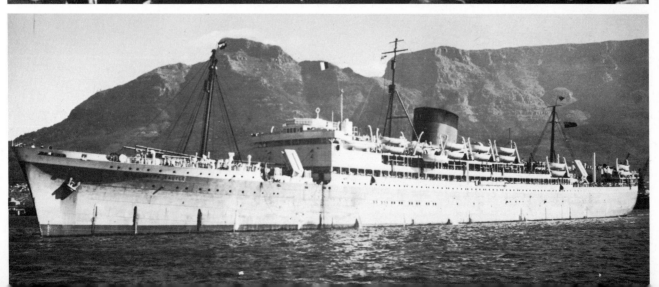

Motorship *Winchester Castle*
Union-Castle Line, London

Builders: Harland & Wolff,
Belfast
Yard no: 825
20,109 GRT; 200.2 × 23.0 m /
657 × 75.5 ft; Burmeister & Wain
diesel; H & W; Twin screw; 15,000
BHP; 16, max 18 kn; Passengers:
259 1st class; 243 2nd class, 254
3rd class; Crew: 350.

1929 Nov 19: Launched.
1930 Oct: Completed.
Oct 24: Maiden voyage
Southampton-Cape Town.
1938 Rebuilt by Harland & Wolff.
New B & W diesels with 26,000
BHP for 20 knot service speed.
Only one funnel. 20,012 GRT.
Passenger accommodation
modernised.
Dec 19: Trials after rebuilding.
1940 Troop transport.
1941 Training ship for troop
landings, and from 1942 landing-
ship.
1947 Emigrant service to South
Africa as one-class ship for 1,300
passengers.
1948 General overhaul at Harland
& Wolff. 20,001 GRT. Passengers:
189 1st class, 398 tourist class.
Re-entered Southampton-Cape
Town service.
1960 Nov 5: Arrived at Mihara,
Japan. Broken up by Nichimen Co.

Motorship *Warwick Castle*
Union-Castle Line, London

Builders: Harland & Wolff,
Belfast
Yard no: 840
20,445 GRT; 206.4 × 23.0 m /
677 × 75.5 ft; Burmeister & Wain
diesel, H & W; Twin screw; 15,000
BHP; 16, max 18 kn; Passengers:
260 1st class, 245 2nd class, 254
3rd class; Crew: 350.

1930 Apr 29: Launched.
1931 Jan 17: Completed.
Jan 30: Maiden voyage
Southampton-Cape Town.
1938 Rebuilt by Harland & Wolff.
New B & W diesels with 26,000
BHP for 20 knot service speed.
Only one funnel. 20,107 GRT.
Passengers: 262 1st class, 228 2nd
class, 209 tourist class.
Sep 30: Trials after rebuilding.
1939 Troop transport.
1942 Nov 14: During a homeward
voyage from North Africa to
England the *Warwick Castle* was
attacked by the German
submarine *U 413* 200 nautical
miles off Portugal in position
38°44′ N-13°00′ W and sunk by
torpedo. 63 dead.

8 The Winchester Castle *in 1939.*
9/10 The Warwick Castle *in her
original form (9), and as a troop
transport at Cape Town during the
Second World War.*

8

9

10

Motorship *Asturias*
Royal Mail Lines, Belfast

Builders: Harland & Wolff,
Belfast
Yard no: 507
22,071 GRT; 199.8 × 23.9 m /
656 × 78.4 ft; Burmeister & Wain
diesel, H & W; Twin screw; 15,000
BHP; 16, max 17 kn; Passengers:
410 1st class, 232 2nd class, 768
3rd class.

1925 Jul 7: Launched.
1926 Jan 12: Completed.
Feb 27: Maiden voyage
Southampton-La Plata.
1934 Converted to turbine
propulsion by Harland & Wolff.
Geared turbines with 20,000 SHP
for 18, max 19 knots. Forepart
lengthened. Length overall
203.0 m/666 ft. Taller funnels.
22,048 GRT. Passengers: 330 1st
class, 220 2nd class, 768 3rd class.
Sep 24: Trials after refit.
1939 Oct: Armed merchant
cruiser. Forward funnel removed.
1943 Jul 25: The *Asturias* was
torpedoed and badly damaged by
the Italian submarine *Cagni* in the
South Atlantic. The
unmanoeuvrable ship was towed to
Freetown by the Dutch tug
Zwarte Zee and laid up there.
1945 Feb: Having been written off
as a total loss, the *Asturias*
was bought by the British
Admiralty and towed to Gibraltar,
and later to Belfast, for repairs.
Fitted out as troop transport at
Belfast.
1947 Entered service as troop
transport after fitting out. 22,445
GRT. Managed for the Ministry of
Transport by Royal Mail Lines.
1949 Jul 26: First voyage in
emigrant service Southampton-
Sydney.
1953 Troop transport again.
1957 Sep 14: Arrived at Faslane to
be broken up.

1/2 The Asturias *in 1935, after the
funnels had been lengthened during
the conversion to turbine propulsion
(1). In 1939 the ship was fitted out as a
troop transport.*

Motorship *Alcantara*
Royal Mail Lines, Belfast

1958 Kaisho Maru

Builders: Harland & Wolff, Belfast
Yard no: 586
22,181 GRT; 199.8 × 23.9 m / 656 × 78.4 ft; Burmeister & Wain diesel, H & W; Twin screw; 15,000 SHP; 16, max 17 kn; Passengers: 432 1st class, 223 2nd class, 775 3rd class.

1926 Sep 23: Launched.
1927 Feb 18: Completed.
Mar 4: Maiden voyage Southampton-La Plata.
1934 Nov: To Harland & Wolff, Belfast, for rebuilding. New geared turbines with 20,000 SHP for 18, max 19 knots. Taller funnels. Forepart lengthened. 203.0 m / 666 ft length overall. 22,209 GRT.

Passengers: 331 1st class, 220 2nd class, 768 3rd class.
1935 May 4: First voyage after rebuilding work.
1939 Sep 27: Armed merchant cruiser. Forward funnel removed.
1940 Jul 28: The *Alcantara* was badly damaged in a battle with the German auxiliary cruiser *Thor* in the South Atlantic, and was forced to put into Rio de Janeiro.
1943/44 Fitted out at Birkenhead as troop transport.
1944 Mar 14: First voyage as troopship.
1947/48 Overhauled and refitted by Harland & Wolff. 22,608 GRT. Passengers: 221 1st class, 185 2nd class, 470 3rd class.
1948 Oct 8: First post-war voyage Southampton-La Plata.
1958 May: Sold to Japanese breakers.

Jun: Renamed *Kaisho Maru* for the voyage to Japan.
Sep 30: Arrived at Osaka.

3-5 *The three rebuilding stages of the Alcantara: (3), external appearance as a motorship, (4), after the refit as a turbine steamer, and (5), after 1948. The forward funnel was removed in 1939.*

3

The Ile de France

Turbine steamer *Ile de France*
CGT, Le Havre

1959 Furanzu Maru

Builders: Penhoët, St Nazaire
Yard no: R 5
43,153 GRT; 241.3 × 28.0 m /
792 × 91.9 ft; Geared turbines,
Penhoët; Quadruple screw; 60,000
SHP; 23.5, max 24 kn; Passengers:
537 1st class, 603 2nd class, 646
3rd class; Crew: 800.

1926 Mar 14: Launched.
1927 May 29: Completed.
Jun 22: Maiden voyage Le
Havre-New York.
1932 Nov: Refit of passenger
accommodation commenced,
which lasted until April 1933. 670
1st class, 408 2nd class, 508 tourist
class. 43,450 GRT.
1939 Sep: Laid up at New York.

1940 Troop transport to
Indo-China.
Jun: At the time of the French
capitulation the *Ile de France* was
at Singapore.
Jul: Taken over by the British.
Became an Allied troop transport
with a French crew, under
Cunard-White Star management.
1945 Sep 22: Handed back to
France, but continued in troop
transport and repatriation service.
1946 Feb 3: Returned to CGT.
Oct 22: First post-war passenger
voyage Cherbourg-New York.
1947 Apr: Went to St. Nazaire.
Overhauled and rebuilt by Penhoët
Passenger accommodation: 541 1st
class, 577 cabin class, 227 tourist
class. 44,356 GRT. Funnels
reduced to two.
1949 Jul 21: First voyage after

rebuilding work, Le Havre-New
York.
1953 Sep 20: In the North
Atlantic, the *Ile de France* rescued
the crew of the sinking Liberian
cargo vessel *Greenville*.
1956 Jul 26: The *Ile de France*
rescued 753 people from the
Italian liner *Andrea Doria*, sinking
after collision with the Swedish
motorship *Stockholm*.
1958 Dec 11: Sold to Yamamoto
& Co, Osaka, to be broken up.
1959 Feb 26: Last voyage from Le
Havre. Renamed *Furanzu Maru*
for the voyage.
Apr 9: Arrived at Osaka.

1/2 CGT liner Ile de France *as a troop
transport in 1946 (1) and after being
rebuilt in 1949 (2).*
3 The Furanzu Maru *ex* Ile de France
on her way to Osaka, her last voyage.

1

Motorship *Shropshire*
Bibby Line, Liverpool

1939 Salopian

Builders: Fairfield, Glasgow
Yard no: 619
10,560 GRT; 153.0 × 18.4 m /
502 × 60.4 ft; Sulzer diesel,
Fairfield; Twin screw; 7,700 BHP;
15.5 kn; Passengers: 276 1st class;
Crew: 200.

1926 Jun 10: Launched.
Oct 7: Completed.
Liverpool-Rangoon service.
1934 10,519 GRT. From 1938,
10,549 GRT.
1939 Sep: Armed merchant
cruiser. Renamed *Salopian*.
1941 May 13: Attacked by
German submarine *U 98* 400
nautical miles southeast of Cape
Farewell in position 59°04′ N-
38°15′ W. After missing three
times the submarine hit the
Salopian with two torpedoes. The
ship sank two hours later after
three further torpedo hits.

Motorship *Cheshire*
Bibby Line, Liverpool

Builders: Fairfield, Glasgow
Yard no: 620
10,560 GRT; 153.0 × 18.4 m /
502 × 60.4 ft; Sulzer diesel,
Fairfield; Twin screw; 7,700 BHP;
15.5 kn; Passengers: 275 1st class;
Crew: 200.

1927 Apr 20: Launched.
Jul: Completed.
Liverpool-Rangoon service.
1934 10,520 GRT. From 1938,
10,552 GRT.
1939 Oct 30: Commissioned at
Calcutta as armed merchant
cruiser.
1940 Oct 14: The *Cheshire* was
torpedoed by the German
submarine *U 137* northwest of
Ireland, but was able to reach
Liverpool. In service again after six
months.
1942 Aug 18: The *Cheshire* was
torpedoed once more by a German
submarine, this time by the *U 214*

in the Atlantic. Again, she
managed to reach home.
1943 May: Troop transport after
repair and fitting out.
1948 Oct 5: Returned to Bibby
Line.
Overhauled and refitted as
emigrant ship at Liverpool. 650
passengers. 10,623 GRT.
1949 Aug 9: First voyage
Liverpool-Sydney.
1953 Feb: Troop transport again.
1957 Feb 10: Laid up at Liverpool.
Jul 11: Arrived at Newport, Mon.
Broken up by British Iron & Steel
Corp.

1 *The* Shropshire, *sunk in 1941 while
serving as an armed merchant cruiser.*

1

2/3 *The Bibby liner* Cheshire *in the
'30s (2) and after her refit in 1949 (3).*

Motorship *Staffordshire*
Bibby Line, Liverpool

1959 *Stafford Maru*

Builders: Fairfield, Glasgow
Yard no: 630
10,654 GRT; 153.0 × 19.0 m /
502 × 62.3 ft; Sulzer diesel,
Fairfield; Twin screw; 7,700 BHP;
15.5 kn; Passengers: 273 1st class;
Crew: 200.

1928 Oct 29: Launched.
1929 Jan: Completed.
Feb 22: Maiden voyage Liverpool-
Rangoon.
1934 10,595 GRT. From 1938,
10,613 GRT, and from 1940,
10,683 GRT.
1941 Mar 28: The *Staffordshire*
was damaged by German
long-range bombers off the
Scottish coast and had to be
beached. After salvage, repaired
on the Tyne.
1942 Jan: Troop transport. 10,701
GRT.
1948 Nov: Back to Bibby Line.
Rebuilt by Fairfield. Second mast
removed; third and fourth masts
replaced by derricks. New funnel.
10,018 GRT. 109 1st class
passengers.
1950 Re-entered
Liverpool-Rangoon service.
1959 Sold to Mitsui Bussan
Kaisha, Osaka, to be broken up.
Renamed *Stafford Maru* for the
voyage to Osaka.
Oct: Arrived at Osaka.

Motorship *Worcestershire*
Bibby Line, Liverpool

1961 *Kannon Maru*

Builders: Fairfield, Glasgow
Yard no: 640
11,453 GRT; 153.0 × 19.5 m /
502 × 64.0 ft; Sulzer diesel,
Fairfield; Twin screw: 8,200 SHP;
15.5, max 17 kn; Passengers: 286
1st class; Crew: 200.

1930 Oct 8: Launched.
1931 Feb 5: Completed.
Mar 6: Maiden voyage Liverpool-
Rangoon.
1934 11,376 GRT. 1937, 11,402
GRT.
1939 Nov: Armed merchant
cruiser.
1941 Apr 3: The *Worcestershire*
was torpedoed by the German
submarine *U 74* in the North
Atlantic while escorting a convoy,
but managed to remain afloat.
Repairs lasted until December
1941.
1943 Jun: Troop transport.
1947 Oct: Back to Bibby Line.
Refit by Fairfield. 10,329 GRT.
115 1st class passengers.
1949 Liverpool-Rangoon service
again.
1961 Sold to be broken up to C.
Itoh & Co, Osaka.
Renamed *Kannon Maru* for the
voyage to Osaka.
Dec: Arrived at Osaka.

4 *The* Staffordshire, *built for the
Liverpool-Rangoon service. The photograph was taken about 1938.*
5/6 *The external appearance of the*
Worcestershire *in the '30s (5) and after
the refit completed in 1949.*

4

5

6

Turbine steamer *Malolo*
Matson Nav Co, San Francisco

1937 *Matsonia*
1949 *Atlantic*
1954 *Queen Frederica*

Builders: Cramp, Philadelphia
Yard no: 509
17,232 GRT; 177.3 × 25.4 m /
582 × 83.3 ft; Geared turbines,
Cramp; Twin screw; 25,000 SHP;
21, max 22 kn; Passengers: 693 1st
class.

1926 Jun 26: Launched.
1927 May 24: Trials.
May 25: The *Malolo* collided with
the Norwegian steamer *Jacob
Christensen* in fog near Nantucket
and was kept afloat only with great
difficulty. The liner was towed to
New York, having shipped 7,000
tons of water.
Oct: Delivered.
Nov 16: Maiden voyage San
Francisco-Honolulu.
1937 Renamed *Matsonia*.
Passenger accommodation
modernised. 17,226 GRT.
1942 Feb: US Navy transport.
1946 Apr: Released from naval

service.
May 22: After overhaul, San
Francisco-Honolulu service again.
1948 Sold to Home Lines,
Panama, (registered for
Mediterranean Lines until 1953).
Refitted at Ansaldo, Genoa.
Passengers: 349 1st class, 203
cabin class, 626 tourist class.
Panama displacement: 15,602
GRT.
1949 Renamed *Atlantic*.
May 14: First voyage Genoa-New
York.
1952 Feb 29:Southampton-
Halifax service.
20,553 GRT.
Apr 21: First voyage
Southampton-Quebec.
1954 Dec: Renamed *Queen
Frederica*. Passenger accom-
modation altered: 132 1st class,
116 cabin class, 931 tourist
class.
1955 Jan 29: First voyage Piraeus-
New York.
Registered at Piraeus as *Vasilissa
Freideriki*. This Greek equivalent
of *Queen Frederica* was never
painted on the ship which

continued to sail under the original
name.
1955 Apr 23: First voyage Quebec-
Southampton.
1957 Aug 12: First voyage Le
Havre-Montreal.
1960 Sep 8: First voyage
Cuxhaven-Montreal.
1960/61 Refitted at Genoa.
21,329 GRT. Passengers: 174 1st
class, 1,005 tourist class.
1965 Nov: Sold to Dimitri
Chandris, Piraeus. Registered for
Themistocles Nav SA. Placed in
service on Southampton-Australia
route, and used for cruising.
1966 16,435 GRT.
1971 Sep 22: Laid up on River
Dart.
1972 Jun: Went to Piraeus; laid
up there.
1973 Mediterranean cruises.

1/2 The Malolo *in the '20s (1), and
after her 1937 refit (2).*
3 The Queen Frederica *ex* Malolo *after
the 1949 refit.*
*4 The ship was refitted again in
1960/61. She is shown here as a
Chandris cruise liner.*

1

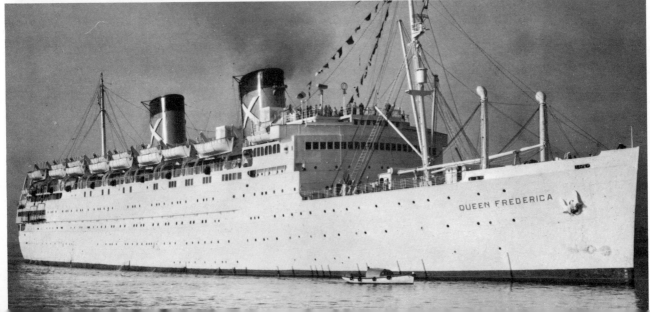

The Blue Star Line A-Class

Turbine steamer *Almeda*
Blue Star Line, London

1929 Almeda Star

Builders: Cammell Laird,
Birkenhead
Yard no: 919
12,838 GRT; 163.1 × 20.8 m /
535 × 68.2 ft; Geared turbines
from builders; Twin screw; 8,400
SHP; 16 kn; Passengers: 180 1st
class.

1926 Jun 29: Launched.
Dec 2: Completed.
1927 Feb 16: Maiden voyage
London-La Plata.
1929 May: Renamed *Almeda
Star*.
1935 Forepart lengthened and
other alterations. 14,935 GRT.
181.9 m /597 ft length overall.
Passengers: 150 1st class.
1941 Jan 17: The *Almeda Star* was
attacked by the German
submarine *U 96* 350 nautical miles
west of the Hebrides. The ship was
able to evade the first three
torpedoes, the first of which was
fired at 07.45 hours. The fourth
one struck, however, and the

Almeda Star sank six hours later
after three further torpedo hits in
position 58°16′ N-13°40′ W. Not
one of the 194 passengers and 166
crew members survived.

Turbine steamer *Andalucia*
Blue Star Line, London
Launched as *Andalusia*

1929 Andalucia Star

Builders: Cammell Laird,
Birkenhead
Yard no: 920
12,846 GRT; 163.1 × 20.8 m /
535 × 68.2 ft; Geared turbines
from builders; Twin screw; 8,400
SHP; 16 kn; Passengers: 180 1st
class.

1926 Sep 21: Launched.
1927 Mar 1: Completed.
Placed into London-La Plata
service.
1929 May: Renamed *Andalucia
Star*.
1937 Forepart lengthened and
other alterations. 14,943 GRT.
181.9 m /597 ft length overall.
Passengers: 150 1st class.
1942 Oct 7: The *Andalucia Star*
was torpedoed and sunk by the
German submarine *U 107* 400
nautical miles west of Monrovia in
position 06°38′ N-15°46′ W.
Four dead. (Date of sinking by
British time: October 6).

1

1 *The prototype of the class, the*
Almeda.

2/3 *The* Andalucia Star *before (2) and*
(3) after the rebuilding work carried
out in 1937.

Turbine steamer *Avila*
Blue Star Line, London

1929 *Avila Star*

Builders: Brown, Clydebank
Yard no: 514
12,872 GRT; 163.1 × 20.8 m /
535 × 68.2 ft; Geared turbines,
Brown; Twin screw; 8,400 SHP; 16
kn; Passengers: 162 1st class.

1926 Sept 22: Launched.
1927 Mar 10: Completed.
Placed in London-La Plata service.
1929 May: Renamed *Avila Star*.
1935 Forepart lengthened and
other alterations. 14,443 GRT.
181.9 m /597 ft length overall. 150
1st class passengers.
1942 Jul 6: The *Avila Star* was
torpedoed and sunk by the
German submarine *U 201* in the
Atlantic in position 38°04′ N–
22°46′ W. 62 dead. (Date of
sinking by British time: July 5).

Turbine steamer *Avelona*
Blue Star Line, London

1929 *Avelona Star*

Builders: Brown, Clydebank
Yard no: 515
12,858 GRT; 163.1 × 20.8 m /
535 × 68.2 ft; Geared turbines,
Brown; Twin screw; 8,400 SHP; 16
kn; Passengers: 162 1st class.

1926 Dec 6: Launched.
1927 May 6: Completed.
May 20: Maiden voyage London-
La Plata.
1929 May: Renamed *Avelona
Star*.
1934 Rebuilt as cargo vessel.
Upper decks and second funnel
removed. 13,376 GRT.
1940 Jun 30; The *Avelona Star*
was torpedoed by the German
submarine *U 43* in the North
Atlantic in position 46°46′ N–
12°17′ W and sank on the
following day. Four dead.

4/5 *Two photographs of the* Avila *later
the* Avila Star *(5) which give a very
clear impression of the rebuilding work
carried out on the first three ships of
the A-Class during the years 1935/37.*

6 *In contrast to her sister-ships, which
continued to carry passengers after
they had been refitted, the* Avelona
Star *was from 1934 purely a cargo
vessel.*

4

5

6

Turbine steamer *Arandora*
Blue Star Line, London

1929 Arandora Star

Builders: Cammell Laird,
Birkenhead
Yard no: 921
12,847 GRT; 163.1 × 20.8 m /
535 × 68.2 ft; Geared turbines
from builders; Twin screw; 8,400
SHP; 16 kn; Passengers: 164 1st
class.

1927 Jan 4: Launched.
May: Completed.
Entered London-La Plata service.
1928/29 Refitted as cruise liner by
Fairfield. 14,694 GRT. 354 1st
class passengers.
1929 May: Renamed *Arandora
Star*.

Jun 15: First cruise Immingham-
Norway.
1931 Jan: White hull.
1934 Oct-Dec: Refitted again at
Southampton. 15,305 GRT.
1936 Rebuilt. Mainmast removed.
Superstructure extended to poop.
15,501 GRT.
1939 Dec: Naval service as
experimental ship for anti-torpedo
nets.
1940 May: Troop transport.
Jul 1: The *Arandora Star* left
Liverpool for Canada, carrying
1,178 German and Italian
internees and prisoners of war,
together with 430 crew and
a military guard. On the
morning of July 2 the unescorted
Arandora Star was 75 nautical
miles west of Bloody Foreland,

Ireland, when she was struck in
the engine room by a torpedo from
the German submarine *U 47*.
Panic broke out among the
prisoners on the sinking ship,
which delayed the lowering of the
boats and rafts. The liner sank one
hour after being hit. 761 people
died: 148 Britons, 143 Germans
and 470 Italians. The survivors
were sighted the same morning by
a Sunderland flying boat and were
later picked up by the Canadian
destroyer *St. Laurent*.

*7-9 The fifth and last ship of the class,
the* Arandora Star, *originally looked
exactly like the* Avila. *In 1929 she was
refitted for cruising. The photographs
show the liner in 1935 (7/8) and in her
final form after 1936 (9).*

7

8

9

Turbine steamer *Roma*
Navigazione Generale Italiana,
Genoa

1943 *Aquila*

Builders: Ansaldo, Sestri Ponente
yard no: 277
32,583 GRT; 216.1 × 25.2 m /
709 × 82.7 ft; Geared turbines,
Ansaldo; Quadruple screw; 44,000
SHP; 22, max 24 kn; Passengers:
375 1st class, 600 2nd class, 700
3rd class; Crew: 510.

1926 Feb 26: Launched.
Sep: Completed.
Sep 21: Maiden voyage Genoa-
New York.
1932 Jan 2: NGI amalgamated
with Lloyd Sabaudo and Cosulich
to form 'Italia' Flotta Riunite,
which went under the name of
'Italia' SAN from 1937.

1939 Laid up. Machinery
alterations planned for higher
speed.
1940 Oct: The *Roma* was taken
over by the Italian Navy, which
ordered her conversion to an
aircraft carrier. Turbines fitted for
a speed of 30 knots.
1943 Renamed *Aquila*.
Sep: The almost completed
aircraft carrier was taken over by
the Germans.
1944 Jun 20: Badly damaged by
several direct hits in an Allied air
raid on Genoa.
1945 Apr 19: The *Aquila* was
attacked and sunk in the harbour
of Genoa by Italian one-man
torpedoes. This prevented the
Germans from sinking the ship to
block the harbour entrance, as had
been feared they might do.

1946 The wreck was raised and
towed to La Spezia.
1951 Scrapped.

1

2

3

4

1 *The* Roma's *original exterior appearance as an NGI liner.*
2/3 *The* Roma *as an 'Italia' liner.*
4 *The aircraft carrier* Aquila *ex* Roma.

Motorship *Augustus*
Navigazione Generale Italiana,
Genoa

1943 *Sparviero*

Builders: Ansaldo, Sestri Ponente
Yard no: 282
32,650 GRT; 216.6 × 25.2 m /
711 × 82.7 ft; MAN diesel, Cant
Officine Savoia; Quadruple screw;
28,000 BHP; 19, max 20 kn;
Passengers: 302 1st class, 504 2nd
class, 1,404 3rd class; Crew: 500.

1926 Dec 13: Launched.
1927 Oct: Completed.
Nov 10: Maiden voyage Genoa-La
Plata ports.
1928 Aug 28: First voyage Genoa-
New York.
1932 Jan 2: NGI amalgamated
with Lloyd Sabaudo and Cosulich
to form 'Italia' Flotta Riunite,
which went under the name of
'Italia' SAN from 1937.

The *Augustus* was used mainly on
the North Atlantic route, but
occasionally for the South
America service and cruising.
1934 Passenger accommodation
altered: 210 1st class, 604 2nd
class, 454 tourist class, 766 3rd
class. 30,418 GRT.
1939 Laid up. Conversion to
turbine propulsion planned in
order to increase speed.
1943 Taken over by the Italian
Navy. Conversion to aircraft
carrier commenced. Renamed
Sparviero, after the name *Falco*
had been considered.
Sep: Taken over by the Germans
after the Italian capitulation.
Conversion work stopped.
1944 Sep 25: Sunk by the
Germans at Genoa in order to
block the harbour.
1946 Wreck raised.
1947 Jul: Sold to be broken up.

5

5/6 *Two photographs of the* Augustus
*in the colours of Navigazione Generale
Italiana.*
7 *The* Augustus, *shown here flying the
'Italia' flag, was the largest passenger
motorship ever built.*

6

7

Motorship *Orazio*
Navigazione Generale Italiana,
Genoa

Builders: Cant ed Officine
Meridionali, Baia
Yard no: 14
11,669 GRT; 154.2 × 18.8 m /
506 × 61.7 ft; Burmeister & Wain
diesel, Stabilimento Tecnico; Twin
screw; 6,600 BHP; 14, max 15 kn;
Passengers: 110 1st class, 190 2nd
class, 340 3rd class; Crew: 200.

1926 Oct 31: Launched.
1927 Oct: Completed.
Entered Genoa-Valparaiso service.
1932 Jan 2: Joined 'Italia' Flotta
Riunite in the amalgamation of
NGI with Lloyd Sabaudo and
Cosulich. 'Italia' SAN from 1937.
1940 Jan 21: While carrying 645
people on a voyage from Genoa to
Barcelona the *Orazio* caught fire
off the French coast. The fire was
impossible to control and so the
Orazio radioed an SOS. Some
French destroyers and the Italian
liners *Colombo* and *Conte
Biancamano* hurried to the scene.
The rescue of the passengers and
crew from the burning vessel was
made exceptionally difficult by
bad weather. The master, the last
survivor, was able to leave the ship
during the night of January 21/22.
106 people died in the blaze.

Motorship *Virgilio*
Navigazione Generale Italiana,
Genoa

Builders: Cant ed Officine
Meridionali, Baia
Yard no: 15
11,718 GRT; 154.2 × 18.8 m /
506 × 61.7 ft; Burmeister & Wain
diesel, Stabilimento Tecnico; Twin
screw; 6,600 BHP; 14, max 15 kn;
Passengers: 110 1st class, 190 2nd
class, 340 3rd class; Crew: 200.

1926 Dec: Launched.
1928 Apr: Completed.
Genoa-Valparaiso service.
1932 Jan 2: Joined 'Italia' Flotta
Riunite in the amalgamation of
NGI with Lloyd Sabaudo and
Cosulich. 'Italia' SAN from 1937.
1940 Jun 1: Hospital ship.
1943 Sep: Seized at La Spezia by
the Germans after the Italian
capitulation.
Dec: Badly damaged at Toulon in
Allied air raid.
1944 Jun: Blown up by the
Germans before their retreat from
Toulon. The wreck was raised and
scrapped after the war.

8/9 *The motorships* Orazio *and*
Virgilio, *which were built for service to*
the west coast of South America.

Steamship *Commissaire Ramel*
Messageries Maritimes, Dunkirk

Builders: Constructions Navales,
La Ciotat
10,092 GRT; 152.5 × 18.0 m /
500 × 59.1 ft; III exp eng plus low
pressure turbine; Single screw;
5,000 IHP; 13, max 14 kn;
Passengers: 58 1st class, 78 3rd
class, 416 steerage.

1920 Mar 20: Launched.
Completed as cargo steamer. Then
8,308 GRT. Speed: 11 knots.
1926 Converted to passenger
vessel by Constructions Navales,
La Ciotat. Oil-firing. New low
pressure turbine.
Dec: Completed.
1927 Jan 19: First voyage
Marseille-Sydney-Noumea.
1931 10,061 GRT.
1940 Jul: Taken over in Australia
by the British Ministry of War
Transport.
Managed by Shaw, Savill &
Albion.
Sep 20: The *Commissaire Ramel*
was intercepted in the Indian
Ocean by the German auxiliary
cruiser *Atlantis*. When the
stationary steamer tried to radio a
distress signal she was fired on by
the *Atlantis* and caught fire. Three
men were killed. The rest of the
crew was taken aboard the
auxiliary cruiser which sank the
Commissaire Ramel in position
28°30′ S-74°13′ E.

Motorship *Brazza*
Chargeurs Réunis, Le Havre

Ex *Camranh*

Builders: A et Ch de la Loire,
Nantes
Yard no: 544
10,193 GRT; 144.2 × 18.0 m /
473 × 59.1 ft; Sulzer diesel; Twin
screw; 3,400 BHP; 12, max 13 kn;
Passengers: 179 1st class, 94 2nd
class, 90 3rd class.

1923 Nov 10: Launched as the
Camranh for Chargeurs Réunis.
1924 Dec: Completed as cargo
vessel. Then 8,898 GRT.
1925 Jan: Maiden voyage to South
America.
Jul 10: First voyage Marseille-Indo-
China.
1927 Converted at Nantes to
a passenger ship for West Africa
service. Renamed *Brazza*.
1936 Rebuilt by A et Ch de France
at Dunkirk. New Sulzer diesel
producing 10,800 BHP for 16,
max 17.73 knots. Forepart
extended, 150.1 m/492 ft length
overall. 10,387 GRT.
1940 May 28: The *Brazza* was
torpedoed and sunk by the
German submarine *U 37* 100
nautical miles west of Oporto, in
position 42°43′ N-11°00′ W.

1 *The* Commissaire Ramel *was
converted in 1926 from a cargo to
passenger vessel.*
2 *The* Brazza *was launched in 1923 as
the* Camranh, *the first motorship built
in France. In 1927 she was converted
to a passenger vessel.*

Steamship *Foucauld*
Chargeurs Réunis, Le Havre

Ex *Hoedic*

Builders: F et Ch de la
Méditerranée, La Seyne
Yard no: 1136
11,028 GRT; 152.6 × 17.9 m /
501 × 58.7 ft; III exp eng from
builders; Twin screw; 7,000 IHP;
14 kn; Passengers: 320 1st class, 80
2nd class, 60 3rd class; Crew: 190.

1922 Dec 21: Launched as the
Hoedic for Chargeurs Réunis.
1923 Completed. Then 9,975
GRT. Passengers: 100 1st class, 40
2nd class, 85 3rd class.
Entered South America service.
1928 Jun 5: The *Hoedic* capsized
while under tow in Le Havre
harbour.
Nov 30: The ship was raised after
difficult salvage work.
1929 Apr: Went to Rotterdam for
repairs and refit by Wilton,
Fijenoord.
1929 Dec: Renamed *Foucauld*

after refit. With new measurement
of 11,028 GRT, an additional
boiler and oil-firing, the ship now
had a speed of 15 knots.
1930 Jan 6: First voyage Le
Havre-West Africa.
1940 Jun 20: The *Foucauld* was
sunk off La Pallice in a German air
raid.

3/4 *The* Hoedic (*3*), *which capsized at
Le Havre in 1928 became the* Foucauld
(*4*) *at Rotterdam in 1929.*
5 *The wreck of the* Foucauld *off La
Pallice.*

3

The Cap Arcona

Turbine steamer *Cap Arcona*
Hamburg-South America Line,
Hamburg

Builders: Blohm & Voss,
Hamburg
Yard no: 476
27,560 GRT; 205.9 × 25.7 m /
676 × 84.3 ft; Geared turbines, B
& V; Twin screw; 28,000 SHP; 20,
max 21 kn; Passengers: 575 1st
class, 275 2nd class, 465 3rd class;
Crew: 630.

1927 May 14: Launched.
Oct 29: Completed.
Nov 19: Maiden voyage Hamburg-
La Plata ports.
1940 Nov 29: The *Cap Arcona*
became an accommodation ship
for the German Navy at
Gotenhafen (Gdynia).
1945 The ship transported 26,000
people to the west in three voyages
during the evacuation of the
German eastern territories.
Apr: 5,000 prisoners from the
Neuengamme concentration camp
were embarked while the ship was
off Neustadt in the Bay of Lübeck.
There were now 6,000 people
aboard, including crew and
guards.
May 3: The *Cap Arcona* was
attacked by British
fighter-bombers and caught fire.
Almost all means of rescue were
destroyed by the rockets and
machine-gun fire from the aircraft.
Panic broke out on board, and
shortly afterwards the *Cap Arcona*
capsized. Although the ship was
lying only a few hundred yards
from the shore, with a third of her
width still out of the water, the
disaster claimed 5,000 lives. The
death of these thousands of
concentration camp prisoners was
all the more tragic since it came at
the hands of those who would have
liberated them only a few days
later.
The wreck was broken up on the
spot after the war.

1

1 *The* Cap Arcona *during trials.*
2/3 *The Hamburg-South America flagship during the '30s.*
4 *The accommodation ship* Cap Arcona *at Gotenhafen (Gdynia) at the end of 1944.*

Steamship *Albertville*
Compagnie Maritime Belge,
Antwerp

Builders: A et Ch de la Loire,
St Nazaire
Yard no: 260
10,338 GRT; 155.0 × 18.9 m /
509 × 62.0 ft; IV exp eng,
Hawthorn Leslie; Twin screw;
8,500 IHP; 15 kn; Passengers: 178
1st class, 180 2nd class; Crew: 202.

1927 May 31: Launched.
1928 Jan 12: Completed.
Feb 28: Maiden voyage Antwerp-
Matadi.
1931 10,769 GRT.
1936/37 Rebuilt by Mercantile
Marine Eng Co at Antwerp.
Forepart lengthened. Additional
low pressure turbines fitted. Now
only one funnel. 11,047 GRT.
163.6 m /537 ft length overall.
16.5 knots.
1937 Apr: First voyage after
rebuilding work, Antwerp-Matadi.
1940 Jun 11: The *Albertville* was
sunk off Le Havre by German
aircraft.

Steamship *Leopoldville*
Compagnie Maritime Belge,
Antwerp

Builders: Cockerill, Hoboken
Yard no: 623
11,172 GRT; 149.9 × 18.9 m /
492 × 62.0 ft; IV exp eng,
Cockerill; Twin screw; 8,500 IHP;
15 kn; Passengers: 180 1st class,
180 2nd class; Crew: 237.

1928 Sep 26: Launched.
1929 Aug: Completed.
Oct 8: Maiden voyage Antwerp-
Matadi.
1931 11,256 GRT.
1936/37 Rebuilt by Mercantile
Eng Co at Antwerp. Forepart
lengthened. Additional pressure
turbines fitted. Now only one
funnel. 11,509 GRT. 157.5 m /
517 ft length overall. 16.5 knots.
1937 Jan: First voyage after
rebuilding work, Antwerp-Matadi.
1940 Jul: The *Leopoldville* became
a troop transport under the control
of the British Ministry of War
Transport.
1944 Dec 24: While on a voyage
from Southampton to Cherbourg
with 2,200 American troops on
board, the *Leopoldville* was
torpedoed five nautical miles from
her destination by the German
submarine *U 486*. The ship
remained afloat and dropped
anchor. 45 minutes later the troops
began to leave the ship in the
lifeboats. The British destroyer
Brilliant took over 1,000 people
aboard and sailed for Cherbourg.
Those remaining on board were to
have been taken in a second trip.
An hour later the steamer's
bulkhead suddenly broke. The
Leopoldville sank in ten minutes in
position 49°45′ N-01°34′ W. 808
dead.

*1/2 The original external appearance
of the* Albertville (1) *was considerably
changed by modernisation in 1937 (2).
3/4 The* Albertville's *sister-ship, the*
Leopoldville, *was similarly modernised
in 1937.*

1

The Last White Star Liners

Steamship *Laurentic*
White Star Line, Liverpool

Builders: Harland & Wolff,
Belfast
Yard no: 470
18,724 GRT; 182.9 × 23.0 m /
600 × 75.4 ft; III exp eng plus low
pressure turbine, H & W; 15,000
IHP; 16 kn; Passengers: 594 cabin
class, 406 tourist class, 500 3rd
class.

1927 Jun 16: Launched.
Nov 1: Completed.
Nov 12: Maiden voyage Liverpool-
New York.
1928 Apr 27: First voyage
Liverpool-Montreal.
1934 Cunard Line and White Star
Line amalgamated to form
Cunard-White Star Line.
1935 Aug 18: The ship was
rammed by the Blue Star liner
Napier Star in the Irish Sea. Six of
the *Laurentic's* crew were killed.
Dec: Laid up at Birkenhead.
1936 Sep 14: One voyage to
Palestine as troop transport.
1938 Apr: Laid up at
Southampton and later,
Falmouth.
1939 Aug 24: Armed merchant
cruiser. Probably the last
'deep-sea' coal burner in the Royal
Navy.
1940 Nov 3: The *Laurentic* was
torpedoed off Bloody Foreland,
Ireland, by the German submarine
U 99. After two more torpedo hits
the auxiliary cruiser sank in
position 54°09′ N-13°44′ W on
November 4. 49 dead.

Motorship *Britannic*
White Star Line, Liverpool

Builders: Harland & Wolff,
Belfast
Yard no: 807
26,943 GRT; 217.0 × 25.1 m /
712 × 82.3 ft; Burmeister & Wain
diesel, H & W; Twin screw; 20,000
SHP; 18 kn; Passengers: 504 cabin
class, 551 tourist class, 498 3rd
class; Crew: 500.

1929 Aug 6: Launched.
1930 May 27: First trials.
Jun 21: Delivered.
Jun 28: Maiden voyage Liverpool-
New York.
1934 Cunard Line and White Star
Line amalgamated to form Cunard-
White Star Line.
1935 Apr 19: First voyage
London-New York.
1939 Aug 29: Troop transport.
1947 Mar: Back to Cunard-White
Star Line.
Refit at Liverpool. Passengers: 429
1st class, 564 tourist class. 27,666
GRT.
1948 May 22: First post-war
voyage Liverpool-New York.
1959 27,778 GRT.
1960 Sold to be broken up.
Dec 19: Arrived at Inverkeithing.
1961 Broken up by T.W. Ward.

1 The steamship Laurentic *at the
Hamburg Overseas Landing Stage.
2 The motorships* Britannic (*2*) *and
Georgic were the last ships to be built
for the famous White Star Line. The
keel for a further ship was laid at
Belfast in 1928. Ordered from Harland
& Wolff, yard no 844, this ship was to
have had a displacement of
approximately 60,000 GRT and to
have been named* Oceanic. *Her
silhouette was similar to the outline of
the* Britannic, *but with three funnels.
No decisions had been made on the
type of engines to be used.
Construction got practically no further
than the keel-laying, but the order was
not cancelled until 1930. Until then,
the keel remained on the slipway.*

Motorship *Georgic*
White Star Line, Liverpool

Builders: Harland & Wolff,
Belfast
Yard no: 896
27,759 GRT; 216.7 × 25.1 m /
711 × 82.3 ft; Burmeister & Wain
diesel, H & W; Twin screw; 20,000
SHP; 18 kn; Passengers: 479 cabin
class, 557 tourist class, 506 3rd
class; Crew: 500.

1931 Nov 12: Launched.
1932 Jun 11: Delivered.
Jun 25: Maiden voyage Liverpool-
New York.
1934 Cunard and White Star
amalgamated to form Cunard-
White Star Line.
1935 May 3: First voyage
London-New York.
1939 Sep: Liverpool-New York
service.
1940 Mar: Fitted out on the Clyde
as troop transport.
1941 Jul 14: The *Georgic* was
badly damaged off Port Tewfik in
a German air raid, caught fire and
was beached.
Oct 27: Salvaged.
Dec 29: Commencement of 13-day
voyage to Port Sudan, towed by the
cargo vessels *Clan Campbell* and
City of Sydney.
Temporary repairs carried out.
1942 Mar 31: Arrived at Karachi,
where the *Georgic* had been towed
by the cargo vessels *Haresfield* and
Recorder and the tug *Pauline
Moller*. Further repairs, including
work on the engines, were carried
out here, and from December,
completed at Bombay.
1943 Jan 20: The *Georgic* left
Bombay for Liverpool, whence she
went on to Belfast. Fitted out as
troop transport by Harland &

Wolff. Forward funnel and
mainmast removed. 27,268 GRT.
Sold to Ministry of War Transport,
managed by Cunard-White Star
Line.
1944 Dec: Re-entered service after
fitting out.
1948 Converted on the Tyne to
one-class emigrant ship. 27,469
GRT.
1949 Jan 11: First voyage
Liverpool-Sydney.
1950 May 4: First post-war voyage
Liverpool-New York.
Used alternately in Australia and
North Atlantic service until 1955.
1955 Sold to Shipbreaking
Industries to be broken up.
1956 Feb 1: Arrived at Faslane.

3/4 The Georgic *in the '30s (3) and as
a troop transport after her fitting out
in 1943 (4).*

3

4

Furness Liner Bermuda

Motorship *Bermuda*
Furness, Withy & Co, Hamilton,
Bermuda

Builders: Workman, Clark & Co,
Belfast
Yard no: 490
19,086 GRT; 166.7 × 22.6 m /
547 × 74.1 ft; Doxford diesel;
Quadruple screw; 14,500 BHP; 17,
max 18.25 kn; Passengers: 616 1st
class, 75 2nd class.

1927 Jul 28: Launched.
Dec 14: Completed.
1928 Jan 14: Maiden voyage New
York-Hamilton.
1931 Jun: The *Bermuda's*
superstructure was completely
destroyed by fire at Hamilton.
Jul: To Belfast for repairs.
Nov 19: Shortly before the
completion of repairs fire broke
out again on the *Bermuda*. The
liner burnt out completely and
sank.
Dec 24: The wreck was raised.
1932 May: The *Bermuda* was
bought by Workman, Clark & Co.
Jun: After the still intact engines
had been removed the ship was
sold to Metal Industries Ltd,
Rosyth. On the way to Rosyth,
being towed by the *Seaman*, the
wreck ran aground on the Badcall
Islands in Eddrachilles Bay,
Scotland.

1/2 *The* Bermuda (*1*), *a luxury liner
built for the New York-Bermuda
service, was destroyed by fire at
Hamilton in 1931* (*2*).

1

2

Turbo-electric vessel *California*
American Line, New York

1938 *Uruguay*

Builders: Newport News SB & DD
Co
Yard no: 315
20,325 GRT; 183.2 × 24.5 m /
601 × 80.4 ft; Turbo-electric
drive, General Electric Co; Twin
screw; 17,000 SHP; 17, max 18.5
kn; Passengers: 384 1st class, 363
tourist class; Crew: 350.

1927 Oct 1: Launched.
1928 Jan 7: Completed.
Jan 28: Maiden voyage New York-
San Francisco.
1934 17,833 GRT.
1937 Sold to US Maritime
Commission. Rebuilt for South
America service. Only one funnel.
20,183 GRT. 500 passengers.
1938 Renamed *Uruguay*. New
York-Buenos Aires service under
company name of American
Republic Line, managed by Moore
& McCormack, New York.
1942 Jan: Troop transport for
War Shipping Administration.
1943 13 people were killed on the
Uruguay in a collision with a US
Navy tanker off Bermuda.
1946/47 Overhauled and refitted
for South America service. 20,237
GRT.
1947 New York-La Plata service
again, now carrying the funnel
markings of Moore-McCormack
Lines.
1954 Laid up on the James River.
US Reserve Fleet.
1963 Nov 21: Sold to the North
American Smelting Co,
Wilmington, Del, to be broken up.
1964 Mar: Arrived at
Bordentown, NJ.

Turbo-electric vessel *Virginia*
American Line, New York

1938 *Brazil*

Builders: Newport News SB & DD
Co
Yard no: 326
20,773 GRT; 186.8 × 24.5 m /
613 × 80.4 ft; Turbo-electric
drive, General Electric Co; Twin
screw; 17,000 SHP; 17, max 18.5
kn; Passengers: 385 1st class, 365
tourist class; Crew: 350.

1928 Oct 18: Launched.
Dec: Completed.
Dec 6: Maiden voyage New
York-San Francisco.
1933 18,298 GRT.
1937 Sold to Maritime
Commission. Rebuilt for South
America service. Only one funnel.
500 passengers.
1938 Renamed *Brazil*. 20,614
GRT. New York-Buenos Aires
service in the colours of the
American Republic Line, managed
by Moore & McCormack, New
York.
1942 Troop transport for the War
Shipping Administration.
1946 Refitted for passenger
service.
1947 New York-La Plata service
for Moore-McCormack Lines.
20,683 GRT.
1960 Laid up.
1964 Jan 28: Arrived at First Steel
& Ship Corp, New York, to be
broken up.

1 *The* California, *the first of three
American Line turbo-electric vessels
built for the New York-San Francisco
service.*
2/3 *The* Virginia *(2) as an American
Liner, and as the* Brazil *in 1940 with
the funnel markings of the American
Republic Line.*

1

2

3

Turbo-electric vessel *Pennsylvania*
American Line, New York

1938 *Argentina*

Builders: Newport News SB & DD
Co
Yard no: 329
20,526 GRT; 186.8 × 24.5 m /
613 × 80.4 ft; Turbo-electric
drive, General Electric Co; Twin
screw; 17,000 SHP; 17, max 18.5
kn; Passengers: 385 1st class, 365
tourist class; Crew: 350.

1929 Jul 10: Launched.
Completed.
New York-San Francisco service.
1933 18,200 GRT.
1937 Sold to the US Maritime
Commission. Rebuilt for South
America service. 500 passengers.
One funnel.
1938 Renamed *Argentina*. 20,164
GRT.
New York-Buenos Aires service in
the colours of the American
Republic Line, managed by Moore
& McCormack.
1942 Troop transport for War
Shipping Administration.
1947 In New York-La Plata
service again for
Moore-McCormack Lines. 20,707
GRT.
1963 Nov 21: Sold to be broken up
to Peck Iron & Metal Co,
Portsmouth, Va.
1964 Sold again to Luria Bros.
Oct: Arrived at South Kearny, NJ,
and broken up there.

4/5 *The* Pennsylvania *in the '30s (4)
and in the '50s as the* Argentina *of
of Moore-McCormack Lines.*

4

5

Turbine steamer *Duchess of Atholl*
Canadian Pacific, London

Builders: Beardmore, Glasgow
Yard no: 648
20,119 GRT; 183.2 × 22.9 m /
601 × 75.1 ft; Geared turbines,
Beardmore; Twin screw; 21,180
SHP; 18, max 19 kn; Passengers:
573 cabin class, 480 tourist class,
510 3rd class; Crew: 518.

1927 Nov 23: Launched.
1928 Jun: Completed.
Jul 7: Cruising Liverpool-Hebrides
Jul 13: Maiden voyage Liverpool-
Montreal.
1939 Dec 30: Troop transport.
1942 Oct 10: The *Duchess of
Atholl* was torpedoed and sunk by
the German submarine *U 178* 200
nautical miles east of Ascension, in
position 07°03′ S-11°12′ W. Four
dead.

Turbine steamer *Duchess of
Bedford*
Canadian Pacific, London

1947 *Empress of India*
1947 *Empress of France*

Builders: Brown, Clydebank
Yard no: 518
20,123 GRT; 183.1 × 22.9 m /
601 × 75.1 ft; Geared turbines,
Brown; Twin screw; 21,000 SHP;
18, max 19 kn; Passengers: 580
cabin class, 480 tourist class, 510
3rd class; Crew: 510.

1928 Jan 24: Launched.
May 12: Completed.
Jun 1: Maiden voyage Liverpool-
Montreal.
1939 Aug 30: First voyage as troop
transport Liverpool-Bombay.
1947 Mar 3: Arrived at Fairfield,
Glasgow, for an overhaul and refit.
Renamed *Empress of India*.
Oct: Renamed *Empress of France*.

1948 Sep 1: First post-war voyage
Liverpool-Montreal. 20,448 GRT.
Passengers: 400 1st class, 300
tourist class.
1958/59 New streamlined funnels.
Passengers: 218 1st class, 482
tourist class.
1960 Sold to be broken up to
British Iron & Steel Corp.
Dec 22: Arrived at Newport, Mon.
Broken up by J. Cashmore.

1 *The* Duchess of Atholl, *sunk in 1942
by a German submarine.*
2/3 *The* Duchess of Bedford (2)
became the Empress of France *in
1947/48.*
4 *In 1959 the funnels on the* Empress
of France *were streamlined.*

1

2

3

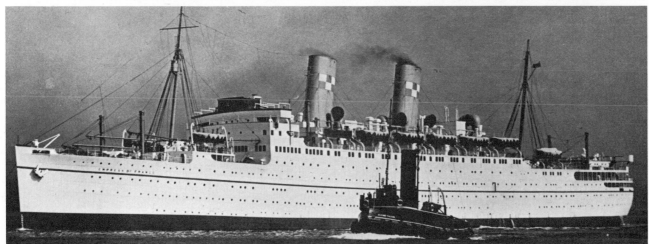

4

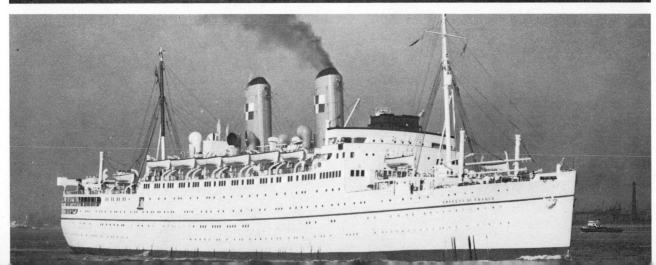

Turbine steamer *Duchess of Richmond*
Canadian Pacific, London

1947 *Empress of Canada*

Builders: Brown, Clydebank
Yard no: 523
20,022 GRT; 183.1 × 22.9 m /
600 × 75.1 ft; Geared turbines,
Brown; Twin screw; 21,000 SHP;
18, max 19 kn; Passengers: 580
cabin class, 480 tourist class, 510
3rd class; Crew: 510.

1928 Jun 18: Launched.
Dec 20: Completed.
1929 Jan 26: Cruising Liverpool-
Canary Islands-Africa.
Mar 15: Maiden voyage Liverpool-
St. John.
1940 Jan 7: First voyage as troop
transport Liverpool-Suez.
1946 May: Arrived at Fairfield,
Glasgow. Overhaul and refit.
20,325 GRT. Passengers: 400 1st
class, 300 tourist class.

1947 Jul 12: Renamed *Empress of Canada*.
Jul 16: First post-war voyage
Liverpool-Montreal.
1953 Jan 25: Burnt out at
Liverpool. Heeled over and sank.
1954 Mar 6: The *Empress* was
righted.
Jun 30: Wreck raised and towed
into the Gladstone dry-dock.
Aug: Sold to be broken up to Cant
di Portovenere, Genoa.
Oct 10: Arrived at La Spezia, in
tow of the Dutch tug *Zwarte Zee*.

Turbine steamer *Duchess of York*
Canadian Pacific, London

Builders: Brown, Clydebank
Yard no: 524
20,021 GRT; 183.1 × 22.9 m /
601 × 75.1 ft; Geared turbines,
Brown; Twin screw; 21,000 SHP;
18, max 19 kn; Passengers: 580
cabin class, 480 tourist class, 510
3rd class; Crew: 510.

1928 Sep 28: Launched. The
name *Duchess of Cornwall* had
originally been intended.
1929 Mar: Completed.
Mar 22: Maiden voyage Liverpool-
St. John.
1940 Mar 7: Troop transport.
1943 Jul 11: While on a voyage
from Glasgow to Freetown the
Duchess of York was attacked by
German long-range bombers west
of Oporto and set on fire. All but
11 of the crew and troops were
taken aboard the destroyers
Douglas and *Iroquois* and the
frigate *Moyola*.
The burning wreck had to be
abandoned and on the next day
was torpedoed and sunk by a
convoy escort.

5

5 *The turbine steamer* Duchess of
Richmond.
6/7 *The* Empress of Canada (*6*) *ex*
Duchess of Richmond *burned out and
heeled over at Liverpool in January
1953. Picture 7 shows the wreck after it
had been righted.*
8 *The last ship of the class, the*
Duchess of York, *was sunk by German
bombers in 1943.*

6

7

8

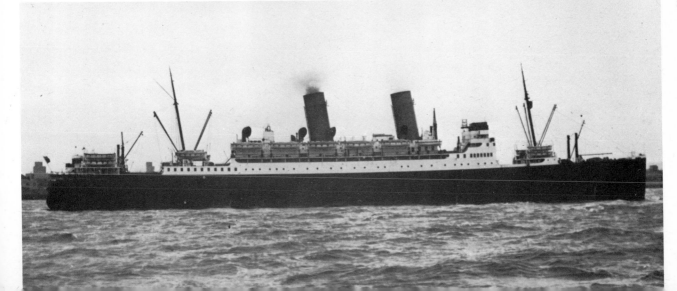

Turbine steamer *Nieuw Holland*
Koninklijke Paketvaart Mij,
Batavia

Builders: Nederlandsche SB Mij,
Amsterdam
Yard no: 187
10,903 GRT; 160.6 × 19.0 m /
527 × 62.3 ft: Geared turbines,
Stork; Twin screw; 8,000 SHP; 15
kn; Passengers: 123 1st class, 50
3rd class; Crew: 199.

1927 Dec 17: Launched.
1928 Apr 20: Completed.
Entered service on Java-Australia
route.
1930 11,057 GRT. From 1938,
11,066 GRT.
1940 Troop transport under
British management. Went back
to original route after the war.
Home port Amsterdam.
1947 Transferred to the new
shipping company Koninkl Java
China Paketvaart Lijnen,
Amsterdam.
1948 11,215 GRT. 155
passengers.
1959 Feb: Sold to be broken up at
Hong Kong.

Turbine steamer *Nieuw Zeeland*
Koninklijke Paketvaart Mij,
Batavia

Builders: Rotterdamsche DD Mij
Yard no: 142c
10,906 GRT; 160.6 × 19.0 m /
527 × 62.3 ft; Geared turbines,
Mij Fijenoord; Twin screw; 8,000
SHP; 15 kn; Passengers: 123 1st
class, 50 3rd class; Crew: 200.

1928 Jan 6: Launched.
Apr 12: Completed.
Placed on Java-Australia service.
1931 11,069 GRT.
1935 Aug: Fitting of new turbines
commenced by Mij Fijenoord,
which lasted until December.
1940 Troop transport under
British management.
1942 Nov 11: The *Nieuw Zeeland*,
which had brought Allied troops to
North Africa, was torpedoed and
sunk by the German submarine
U 407 in the Mediterranean during
her homeward voyage in position
35°57′ N-03°58′ E. 15 dead.

1/2 *The* Nieuw Holland *about 1935 (1)
and in her final years of service (2).*
3 *The KPM liner* Nieuw Zeeland.

1

2

3

The Ausonia

Turbine steamer *Ausonia*
Soc Ital di Servizi Marittimi,
Genoa

Builders: Ansaldo, Sestri Ponente
Yard no: 283
12,955 GRT; 165.8 × 20.2 m /
544 × 66.3 ft; Geared turbines,
Ansaldo; Twin screw; 20,000 SHP;
20, max 21 kn; Passengers: 210 1st
class, 120 2nd class, 60 3rd class;
Crew: 300.

1927 Oct 20: Launched.
1928 Jun: Completed.
Genoa-Alexandria-Venice service.
1931 Joined Lloyd Triestino.
1932 Jan 16: First voyage
Trieste-Alexandria.
1935 Home port Trieste.
Oct 18: Completely burnt out at
Alexandria.
1936 Towed to Trieste and broken
up.

1 *The* Ausonia, *built for the
Mediterranean express service in 1928;
shown here in Lloyd Triestino colours.*

1

Motorship *Highland Monarch*
Nelson Line, Belfast

Builders: Harland & Wolff,
Belfast
Yard no: 751
14,137 GRT; 165.8 × 21.1 m /
544 × 69.2 ft; Burmeister & Wain
diesel, H & W; Twin screw; 10,000
BHP; 15 kn; Passengers: 135 1st
class, 66 2nd class, 500 3rd class.

1928 May 3: Launched.
Sep 24: Completed.
Oct 18: Maiden voyage London-
Buenos Aires.

1932 The Nelson Line ships were
taken over by Royal Mail Lines.
Troop and supply transport during
the Second War War.
1948 Re-entered London-La Plata
service. 14,216 GRT. Passengers:
104 1st class, 335 3rd class.
1960 Apr 28: Arrived at Dalmuir.
Broken up by W. H. Arnott
Young.

1 *Nelson liner* Highland Monarch *was
the prototype of a class of six sister-
ships. In 1932 Royal Mail Lines took
over the Nelson Line.*
2 *The* Highland Monarch *as a Royal
Mail liner.*

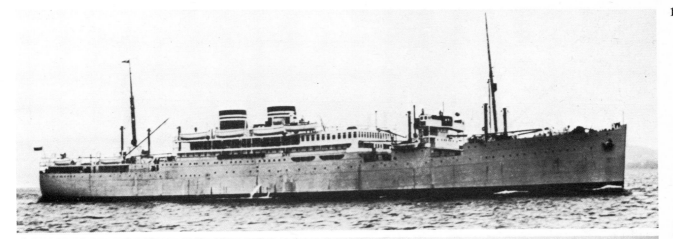

Motorship *Highland Chieftain*
Nelson Line, Belfast

1959 *Calpean Star*

Builders: Harland & Wolff,
Belfast
Yard no: 806
14,131 GRT; 165.8 × 21.1 m /
544 × 69.2 ft: Burmeister & Wain
diesel, H & W; Twin screw; 10,000
SHP; 15, max 16 kn; Passengers:
135 1st class, 66 2nd class, 500 3rd
class.

1928 Jun 21: Launched.
1929 Jan 26: Completed.
Feb 21: Maiden voyage London-
Buenos Aires.
1932 Royal Mail Lines took over
the Nelson Line ships.
Served as troop transport during
the Second World War.
1948 Re-entered London-La Plata
service after overhaul. 14,232
GRT. Passengers: 104 1st class,
335 3rd class.
1959 Oct: Sold to Calpe Shipping
Co Ltd, Gibraltar. Renamed
Calpean Star. Used as
maintenance ship and transport
for whaling fleets in the Antarctic.
1960 Mar: The *Calpean Star* left
the Antarctic with a damaged
rudder for repairs at Montevideo.
Jun 1: After the ship had left
Montevideo, there was an
explosion in the engine room,
which caused her to sink two
nautical miles from the coast.

3/4 *The* Highland Chieftain *was sold
in 1958 and renamed* Calpean Star. *In
1950 the ship sank off Montevideo
after an explosion* (4).

3

4

Motorship *Highland Brigade*
Nelson Line, Belfast

1959 *Henrietta*
1960 *Marianna*

Builders: Harland & Wolff,
Belfast
Yard no: 812
14,131 GRT; 165.8 × 21.1 m /
544 × 69.2 ft; Burmeister & Wain
diesel, H & W; Twin screw; 10,000
SHP; 15, kn; Passengers: 135 1st
class, 66 2nd class, 500 3rd class.

1928 Nov 1: Launched.
1929 Apr 27: Completed.
London-Buenos Aires service.
1932 The Nelson Line ships were
taken over by Royal Mail Lines.
Used as transport during the
Second World War.
1946 Jan: Badly damaged by a

mine off Singapore.
1947 Nov: London-La Plata
service again after repairs. 14,216
GRT. Passengers: 104 1st class,
335 3rd class.
1959 Sold to John S. Latsis,
Piraeus. Renamed *Henrietta*. The
ship was intended for the Genoa-
Australia service, but never
entered it. One funnel was
removed. The *Henrietta* was then
used as a pilgrim carrier in Asian
waters.
1960 Renamed *Marianna*.
1965 Jun 29: Arrived at
Kaohsiung to be broken up.

Motorship *Highland Hope*
Nelson Line, Belfast

Builders: Harland & Wolff, Govan
Yard no: 813G
14,129 GRT; 165.8 × 21.1 m /
544 × 69.2 ft; Burmeister & Wain
diesel, H & W; Twin screw; 10,000
SHP; 15 kn; Passengers: 135 1st
class, 66 2nd class, 500 3rd class;
Crew: 150.

1929 Jan 24: Launched.
1930 Jan 18: Completed.
London-Buenos Aires service.
Nov 19: While sailing from Vigo to
the first Portuguese port of call the
Highland Hope, which was
carrying over 500 people, ran onto
one of the Farilhoes rocks. The
passengers and crew took to the
boats, and the ship had to be
abandoned.

5

5/6 *The* Highland Brigade (*5*) *became the* Marianna (*6*) *in 1960.*
7 *The Nelson liner* Highland Hope, *which stranded off the Farilhoes in 1930.*

Motorship *Highland Princess*
Nelson Line, Belfast

1959 *Marianna*
1960 *Slapy*
1960 *Guanghua*

Builders: Harland & Wolff,
Belfast
Yard no: 814
14,128 GRT; 165.8 × 21.1 m /
544 × 69.2 ft; Burmeister & Wain
diesel, H & W; Twin screw; 10,000
SHP; 15, max 16 kn; Passengers:
135 1st class, 66 2nd class, 500 3rd
class; Crew: 150.

1929 Apr 11: Launched.
1930 Feb 25: Completed.
Entered London-La Plata service.
1932 The Nelson Line ships were
taken over by Royal Mail Lines.
Used as transport during the
Second World War.
1947 London-La Plata service
again after overhaul and refit.
14,216 GRT. Passengers: 102 1st
class, 342 3rd class.

1959 Sold to John S. Latsis,
Piraeus. Renamed *Marianna*.
Intended for Genoa-Australia
service, but never entered it.
1960 Sold to Czechoslovak Ocean
Shipping, Prague. Renamed
Slapy. Sold again in the same year
to the People's Republic of China.
Renamed *Guanghua*.

Motorship *Highland Patriot*
Nelson Line, Belfast

Builders: Harland & Wolff,
Belfast
Yard no: 916
14,130 GRT; 165.8 × 21.1 m /
544 × 69.2 ft; Burmeister & Wain
diesel, H & W; Twin screw; 10,000
SHP; 15, max 16 kn; Passengers:
135 1st class, 66 2nd class, 500 3rd
class; Crew: 150.

1931 Dec 10: Launched.
1932 May 14: Completed.
May 28: Maiden voyage London-
Buenos Aires.
Along with the other Nelson Line
ships, she came under the Royal
Mail Lines flag.
1933 14,157 GRT.
1940 Oct 1: While on a voyage
from Buenos Aires to Glasgow the
Highland Patriot was torpedoed
and sunk by the German
submarine *U 38* 500 nautical miles
west of Bishops Rock in position
52°20′ N-19°04′ W. Three dead.

8

9

10

8/9 *The* Highland Princess (*8*) *sails today under the flag of Red China as the* Guanghua (*9*).
10 *The* Highland Patriot *during trials*.

Motorship *St. Louis*
Hamburg-America Line,
Hamburg

Builders: Bremer Vulkan,
Vegesack
Yard no: 670
16,732 GRT; 174.9 × 22.1 m /
574 × 72.5 ft; MAN diesel,
Vulkan; Twin screw; 12,600 BHP;
16, max 16.5 kn; Passengers: 270
cabin class, 287 tourist class, 416
3rd class; Crew: 330.

1928 Aug 2: Launched.
1929 Mar 21: Completed.
Mar 28: Maiden voyage Hamburg-
New York. Also used for cruising.
1939 May 13: The *St. Louis* left
Hamburg for Cuba, carrying 900
Jewish emigrants. The Cuban
authorities at Havana refused to
accept the emigrants, and the USA
was not prepared to take them.
Hamburg-America Line instructed
the ship to cruise around at sea for
a few weeks, in order to shield the
passengers from the possible
consequences of a return to
Germany. Finally, Belgium,
France, Great Britain and the
Netherlands agreed to grant the
emigrants asylum. On June 17 they
were able to disembark at
Antwerp.
Aug 26: Due to the threat of war
the *St. Louis* left New York
without any passengers and
reached Murmansk on September
11, which she used as a port of
refuge.
1940 Jan 1: Arrived at Hamburg.
The *St. Louis* became a naval
accommodation ship at Kiel.
1944 Aug 30: Badly damaged at
Kiel by three bomb hits.
Sep 2: Beached.
1946 Towed to Hamburg. The

ship was used as a hotel at the
Altona landing-stage until 1950.
1952 Broken up at Bremerhaven.

1

2

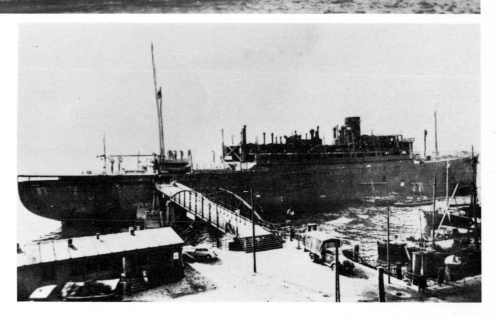

1 *The* St. Louis *was Germany's largest motorship until 1936.*
2 *After the war the partly burnt-out* St. Louis *was used as a hotel ship in Hamburg harbour.*

Motorship *Milwaukee*
Hamburg-America Line,
Hamburg

1945 *Empire Waveney*

Builders: Blohm & Voss,
Hamburg
Yard no: 483
16,699 GRT; 175.1 × 22.1 m /
575 × 72.5 ft; MAN diesel, B & V;
Twin screw; 12,600 BHP; 16, max
16.5 kn; Passengers: 270 cabin
class, 259 tourist class, 428 3rd
class; Crew: 335.

1929 Feb 20: Launched.
Jun 11: Completed.
Jun 18: Maiden voyage Hamburg-
New York.
Cruising.
1935 Refit as cruise ship
commenced by Blohm & Voss
which lasted until the beginning of
1936. 559 1st class passengers.
16,754 GRT.

1940 Naval accommodation ship
at Kiel.
1945 May 9: British war prize.
Renamed *Empire Waveney*. Troop
transport for Ministry of
Transport. Cunard-White Star
management.
1946 Mar 1: The *Empire Waveney*
completely burnt out at Liverpool
while refitting and sank.
May: Raised.
1947 Jan 25: Towed to Glasgow.
Broken up there by Arnott Young.
Sep 25: The hull was towed to
Troon and scrapped.

3/4 *The* Milwaukee (*3*) *had a black
hull until 1934. In 1935/36 the ship
was refitted as a luxury liner with
facilities for Spa-type medical
treatment.*
5 *The* Empire Waveney *ex* Milwaukee
on fire at Liverpool.

3

Motorship *General Osorio*
Hamburg-America Line,
Hamburg

Builders: Bremer Vulkan,
Vegesack
Yard no: 669
11,590 GRT; 160.8 × 20.1 m /
528 × 66.0 ft; MAN diesel,
Vulkan; Twin screw; 8,200 BHP;
15, max 15.5 kn; Passengers: 228
2nd class, 752 3rd class; Crew:
196.

1929 Mar 20: Launched.
Jun 14: Maiden voyage Hamburg-
La Plata ports.
1931 Aug 8: The *General Osorio*
took 88 people aboard from the
American passenger ship *Western
World*, which had run aground off
San Sebastian.
1934 Nov 1: Chartered to
Hamburg-South America Line as
part of the State reorganisation of
German shipping.
1936 Jun 30: Sold to Hamburg-
South America Line.
1940 Apr 10: Naval
accommodation ship at Kiel. Later
served as target ship.
1944 Jul 24: Partly burnt out after
bomb hit at Kiel. The aft section of
the ship was beached.
Oct 2: Raised. Temporarily
repaired.
1945 Apr 9: Sunk by a bomb at
Kiel.
1947 The wreck was raised.
Aug 29: To Great Britain to be
scrapped.

6-8 *Motorship* General Osorio *during
trials, as a Hamburg-South America
liner with lengthened funnels (7) and
painted grey during the war (8).*

6

7

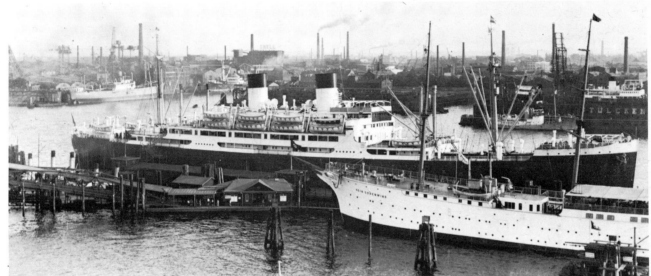

8

Turbine steamer *Europa*
North German Lloyd, Bremen

1946 *Liberté*
Builders: Blohm & Voss,
Hamburg
Yard no: 479
49,746 GRT; 286.7 × 31.1 m /
941 × 102.0 ft; Geared turbines,
B & V; Quadruple screw; 130,000
SHP; 27, max 28.5 kn; Passengers:
687 1st class, 524 2nd class, 306
tourist class, 507 3rd class; Crew:
970.

1928 Aug 15: Launched.
1929 Mar 26: The nearly
completed ship was severely
damaged by a large fire at the
fitting-out wharf. This delayed
delivery by ten months.
1930 Feb 22: Completed.
Mar 19: Maiden voyage
Bremerhaven-New York. Despite
the unfavourable weather
conditions the *Europa* achieved an
average speed of 27.91 knots
between Cherbourg and Ambrose,
thus winning the Blue Riband,
which she held until 1933.

1937 Jan 29: The *Europa* rescued
three men from the German tanker
Olifer, which sank with the loss of
ten lives in a storm in the North
Sea.
1939 Naval accommodation ship
at Bremerhaven.
1940 Transferred to Hamburg,
where the ship was to be fitted out
for the invasion of England. The
refit was not carried out for
reasons of stability. The *Europa*
returned to Bremerhaven.
1942 Detailed plans were worked
out for the conversion of the ship to
an aircraft carrier, but they were
not carried out.
1945 May: Seized by the USA.
Used as US Navy transport on the
North Atlantic.
1946 Jun: Handed over to France.
Awarded to CGT and renamed
Liberté.
Dec 8: During a storm at Le
Havre, where she was laid up, the
Liberté broke away from her
moorings and ran into the wreck of
the overturned French liner *Paris*.
With her hull ripped open, the

Liberté sank.
1947 Apr 15: Raised. Towed to St.
Nazaire. Rebuilt and overhauled
there by Penhoët.
1949 Oct: Reconstruction work
was considerably delayed by a
serious fire in the passenger decks.
1950 51,839 GRT after
completion of refit. Passengers:
569 1st class, 562 cabin class, 382
tourist class.
Aug 17: First voyage Le Havre-
New York.
1961 Dec: Sold to be broken up.
1962 Jan 30: Arrived at La Spezia.
Scrapped by Terrestre Marittima.

1/2 *The* Europa *during trials* (1) *and
after the lengthening of her funnels.*
3 *The* Europa *in 1945 as a transport
under the US flag* (AP 177).
4/5 *The* Liberté *ex* Europa *in 1950* (4)
*and in 1954 after a further lengthening
of the funnels* (5).
6 & 8 *The famous* Bremen *in 1930* (6)
*and after the lengthening of her
funnels.*
7 *The* Europa *in Hamburg harbour in
1932.*

1

2

3

4

5

6

7

8

Turbine steamer *Bremen*
North German Lloyd, Bremen

Builders: Deschimag, AG 'Weser',
Bremen
Yard no: 872
51,656 GRT; 286.0 × 31.1 m /
938 × 102.0 ft; Geared turbines,
Weser; Quadruple screw; 135,000
SHP; 27, max 28.5 kn; Passengers:
800 1st class, 500 2nd class, 300
tourist class, 600 3rd class; Crew:
990.

1928 Aug 16: Launched.
1929 Jun 24: Completed.
Jul 16: Maiden voyage
Bremerhaven-New York. The
Bremen won the Blue Riband with
an average speed of 27.83 knots
between Cherbourg and Ambrose.
On the return voyage, her average
speed between Ambrose and
Eddystone was 27.92 knots.
1933 Jun: After improvements to
the engines and the elimination of
disturbing vibration in the after
section, the *Bremen* beat the
record set up in 1930 for the
westward crossing by the *Europa*,
achieving an average of 28.51
knots. In August 1933 the *Bremen*
lost the Blue Riband to the Italian
Rex.
1937 51,731 GRT.
1939 Aug 28: The *Bremen* entered
New York for the last time.
Because of the political situation
the ship was to return to Germany
without passengers as quickly as
possible after picking up supplies.
This intention was thwarted by the
US authorities, who held the liner
for two days by working to rule.
Aug 30: Left New York. After the
outbreak of war, the *Bremen*
altered course for Murmansk,
where she arrived on September 6.

Dec 10: Left Murmansk for
Bremerhaven, where she arrived
on December 13.
1940 The *Bremen* became a naval
accommodation ship. Like her
sister-ship *Europa* the *Bremen* was
to have been fitted out for the
invasion of England, and sailed to
Hamburg for this purpose. When
the plans were abandoned she
returned to being an
accommodation ship at
Bremerhaven.
1941 Mar 16: As revenge for a box
on the ears, a cabin-boy started a
fire in one of the ship's storerooms
and the ship was completely burnt
out.
The wreck was scrapped at
Bremerhaven.

9 *The* Bremen *received camouflage
paint in 1940.*
10 *The end of the* Bremen.

Motorship *Rangitiki*
New Zealand Line, Plymouth

Builders: Brown, Clydebank
Yard no: 516
16,755 GRT; 168.5 × 21.4 m /
553 × 70.2 ft; Sulzer diesel,
Brown; Twin screw; 10,500 BHP;
15, max 16.13 kn; Passengers: 100
1st class, 86 2nd class, 412 3rd
class.

1928 Aug 29: Launched.
1929 Jan 26: Completed.
Feb 15: Maiden voyage
Southampton-Wellington.
1930 16,698 GRT.
1940 Dec: Troop transport.
1947/48 Refitted by Brown at
Clydebank. New Doxford engines
from Brown. 15.5 knot cruising
speed. Passengers: 121 1st class,
284 tourist class. 16,985 GRT.
1948 Sep 24: First post-war voyage
London-Wellington.
1962 Jul 26: Arrived at Santander
to be broken up.

1 The Rangitiki, *built for the*
Southampton-Wellington service.
2 *New Zealand Liner* Rangitata.
3 The Rangitane *in one of the Panama*
Canal locks.

Motorship *Rangitata*
New Zealand Line, Plymouth

1962 Rang

Builders: Brown, Clydebank
Yard no: 517
16,737 GRT; 168.5 × 21.4 m /
553 × 70.2 ft; Sulzer diesel,
Brown; Twin screw; 10,500 BHP;
15, max 16 kn; Passengers: 100 1st
class, 85 2nd class, 410 3rd class.

1929 Mar 26: Launched.
Oct: Completed.
Nov 22: Maiden voyage
Southampton-Wellington.
1941 Feb: Troop transport.
1948/49 Refitted by Brown,
Clydebank. New Doxford engines
from Brown. 16,969 GRT.
Passengers: 123 1st class, 288
tourist class.
1949 Sep 23: First post-war voyage
London-Wellington.
1962 Sold to Holland to be broken
up. Sold again to Yugoslavia.
Renamed *Rang* for the voyage
there.
Jul 21: Arrived at Split. Broken up
by Brodospas.

Motorship *Rangitane*
New Zealand Line, Plymouth

Builders: Brown, Clydebank
Yard no: 522
16,733 GRT; 168.5 × 21.4 m /
553 × 70.2 ft; Sulzer diesel,
Brown; Twin screw; 10,500 BHP;
15, max 16 kn; Passengers: 100 1st
class, 85 2nd class, 410 3rd class.

1929 May 27: Launched.
Nov: Completed.
Dec 20: Maiden voyage
Southampton-Wellington.
1930 16,712 GRT.
1940 Nov 27: During the
homeward voyage from Wellington
to England via Panama the
Rangitane was intercepted by the
German auxiliary cruisers *Orion*
and *Komet* 320 nautical miles
north of East Cape, New Zealand.
The German ships immediately
shelled the *Rangitane*, which
caught fire. The crew and
passengers abandoned ship, and
the *Komet* then sank the liner with
a torpedo in position 36°48′ S-
175°07′ W. 16 dead. 299 survivors
were taken aboard by the auxiliary
cruisers.

1

Motorship *Asama Maru*
Nippon Yusen KK, Tokyo

Builders: Mitsubishi, Nagasaki
Yard no: 450
16,975 GRT; 177.7 × 21.9 m /
583 × 71.9 ft; Sulzer diesel;
Quadruple screw; 19,100 BHP; 19,
max 21 kn; Passengers: 222 1st
class, 96 2nd class, 504 3rd class;
Crew: 330.

1928 Oct 30: Launched.
1929 Sep 15: Completed.
Oct 10: Maiden voyage
Yokohama-San Francisco.
1937 Sep 2: The *Asama Maru* was
undergoing repairs at the Taikoo
Dockyard, Hong Kong. Because of
a hurricane warning the ship was
moved to a safe anchorage in
Saiwan Bay. However, the force of
the hurricane which reached the
bay shortly afterwards was so great
that the ship's starboard anchor-
chain broke. The port anchor
could not hold either, and the ship
was tossed ashore. The Nippon

Salvage Co was given the difficult
task of refloating the liner. In
order to get the ship off at high
tide, 3,500 tons of material were
removed, including two of the four
main engines.
1938 Mar: The refloating
operation was successful.
Sep 15: First voyage Yokohama-
San Francisco after salvage and
repairs.
1941/42 Taken over by the
Japanese Navy as a transport.
1944 Nov 1: The *Asama Maru* was
torpedoed and sunk by the US
submarine *Atule* 100 nautical
miles south of Pratas Island in the
China sea in position 20°17′ N-
117°08′ E.

Motorship *Tatsuta Maru*
Nippon Yusen KK, Tokyo

1938 *Tatuta Maru*

Builders: Mitsubishi, Nagasaki
Yard no: 451
16,975 GRT; 178.0 × 21.9 m /
584 × 71.9 ft; Sulzer diesel;
Quadruple screw; 20,000 BHP; 19,
max 20.93 kn; Passengers: 220 1st
class, 96 2nd class, 504 3rd class;
Crew: 330.

1929 Apr 12: Launched.
1930 Mar 15: Delivered.
Apr 25: Maiden voyage
Yokohama-San Francisco.
1938 Transliteration of name
changed to *Tatuta Maru*.
1941 Taken over by the Japanese
Navy as a transport.
1943 The *Tatuta Maru* was
torpedoed and sunk by the US
submarine *Tarpon* 42 nautical
miles east of Mikurashima in
position 33°45′ N-140°25′ E.

1

2

3

1 *The sister-ships* Asama Maru *(1) and*
Tatsuta Maru *were built for NYK's*
trans-Pacific service.
2/3 *Two photographs of the* Asama
Maru *stranded off Hong Kong in 1937.*

Motorship *Chichibu Maru*
Nippon Yusen KK, Tokyo

1938 *Titibu Maru*
1939 *Kamakura Maru*

Builders: Yokohama Dock Co
Yard no: 170
17,498 GRT; 178.0 × 22.6 m /
584 × 74.1 ft; Burmeister & Wain
diesel; Twin screw; 20,900 BHP;
19, max 21.48 kn; Passengers: 222
1st class, 95 2nd class, 500 3rd
class; Crew: 323.

1929 May 8: Launched.
1930 Mar 10: Delivered.
Apr 4: Maiden voyage Yokohama-
San Francisco.
1938 17,526 GRT.
Transliteration of name changed
to *Titibu Maru*.
1939 Renamed *Kamakura Maru*.
1941/42 Taken over by Japanese
Navy as a transport. Used at times
as hospital ship.
1943 Apr 28: During a voyage
from Manila to Singapore the
Kamakura Maru was torpedoed
and sunk by the US submarine
Gudgeon southeast of Lagayan in
position 10°18′ N-121°44′ E.

Motorship *Hikawa Maru*
Nippon Yusen KK, Tokyo

Builders: Yokohama Dock Co
Yard no: 177
11,622 GRT; 163.3 × 20.1 m /
536 × 66.0 ft; Burmeister & Wain
diesel; Twin screw; 11,000 BHP;
17, max 18.5 kn; Passengers: 76
1st class, 69 tourist class, 186 3rd
class.

1929 Sep 30: Launched.
1930 Apr: Completed.
May 13: Maiden voyage Kobe-
Seattle.
Hong Kong-Seattle service.
1941 Hospital ship in Japanese
Navy.
1945 American war prize. Troop
transport Japan-USA.
1947 Returned to Nippon Yusen
KK.
1950 Re-entered trans-Pacific
service after overhaul and
modernisation.
1961 Fitted out as floating youth
hostel at Yokohama.

Motorship *Hiye Maru*
Nippon Yusen KK, Tokyo

1938 *Hie Maru*

Builders: Yokohama Dock Co
Yard no: 178
11,622 GRT; 163.3 × 20.1 m /
535.8 × 65.9 ft; Burmeister &
Wain diesel; Twin screw; 11,000
BHP; 17, max 18.5 kn;
Passengers: 75 1st class, 70 tourist
class, 185 3rd class.

1930 Feb 12: Launched.
Aug: Completed.
Aug 23: Maiden voyage Kobe-
Seattle.
Hong Kong-Seattle service.
1938 Transliteration of name
changed to *Hie Maru*.
1942 Taken over by Japanese Navy
as submarine tender.
1943 Oct 1: Supply ship.
Nov 17: The *Hiye Maru* was
torpedoed and sunk by the US
submarine *Drum* 300 nautical
miles northwest of New Ireland, in
position 01°45′ N—148°35′ E.

4 *In contrast to her two half-sisters the*
Chichibu Maru *had only one funnel.*
5/6 Hikawa Maru *(5),* Hiye Maru *(6)*
and Heian Maru *were the three ships*
used in the trans-Pacific service to
Seattle.

4

5

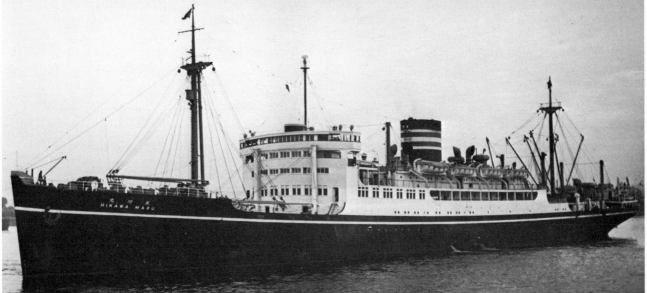

6

Motorship *Heian Maru*
Nippon Yusen KK, Tokyo

Builders: Osaka Iron Works
Yard no: 1128
11,616 GRT; 163.3 × 20.1 m /
535.8 × 65.9 ft; Burmeister &
Wain diesel; Twin screw; 11,000
BHP; 17, max 18.5 kn;
Passengers: 75 1st class, 70 tourist
class, 185 3rd class.

1930 Apr 16: Launched.
Nov: Completed.
Hong Kong-Seattle service.
Dec: Maiden voyage Kobe-Seattle.
1941 Dec 15: Submarine tender in
Japanese Navy.
1944 Feb 17: The *Heian Maru* was
sunk by US aircraft near the Truk
Islands in position 7°35′ N-
151°51′ E.

Motorship *Terukuni Maru*
Nippon Yusen KK, Tokyo

Builders: Mitsubishi, Nagasaki
Yard no: 467
11,930 GRT; 160.5 × 19.5 m /
527 × 64.0 ft; Sulzer diesel,
Mitsubishi; Twin screw; 10,000
BHP; 16.5, max 17.7 kn;
Passengers: 121 1st class, 68 2nd
class, 60 3rd class; Crew: 187.

1929 Dec 19: Launched.
1930 May 31: Delivered.
Yokohama-Hamburg service.
1939 Nov 21: The *Terukuni Maru*
struck a mine in the mouth of the
Thames and sank 45 minutes later.

Motorship *Yasukuni Maru*
Nippon Yusen KK, Tokyo

Builders: Mitsubishi, Nagasaki
Yard no: 468
11,930 GRT; 160.5 × 19.5 m /
527 × 64.0 ft; Sulzer diesel,
Mitsubishi; Twin screw; 10,000
BHP; 16.5, max 17.5 kn;
Passengers: 121 1st class, 68 2nd
class, 60 3rd class; Crew: 187.

1930 Feb 15: Launched.
Aug 31: Delivered.
Yokohama-Hamburg service.
1941 Dec 15: Submarine tender in
the Japanese Navy.
1944 Jan 31: The *Yasukuni Maru*
was torpedoed and sunk by the US
submarine *Trigger* near the Truk
Islands in position 9°12′ N—
147°13′ E.

7/8 *The sister-ships* Terukuni Maru
(*7*) *and* Yasukuni Maru (*8*) *sailed on
the Yokohama-Hamburg route.*

7

8

Motorship *Northern Prince*
Furness, Withy & Co, London

Builders: Lithgows, Pt Glasgow
Yard no: 814
10,917 GRT; 157.3 × 19.7 m /
516 × 64.6 ft; Burmeister & Wain
diesel, Kincaid; Twin screw;
12,000 BHP; 16.5 kn; Passengers;
101 1st class; Crew: 120.

1928 Nov 27: Launched.
1929 Apr 16: Completed.
New York-La Plata service.
1941 Apr 3: While sailing to
Greece in a reinforcements convoy
the *Northern Prince* was sunk by
German aircraft in the Straits of
Kithira.

Motorship *Eastern Prince*
Furness Withy & Co, London

1950 *Empire Medway*

Builders: Napier & Miller,
Glasgow
Yard no: 266
10,926 GRT; 157.3 × 19.7 m /
516 × 64.6 ft; Burmeister & Wain
diesel, Kincaid; Twin screw;
12,000 BHP; 16.5 kn; Passengers:
102 1st class; Crew: 120.

1929 Jan 29: Launched.
Jun: Completed.
New York-La Plata service.
1932 Jan: The *Eastern Prince* took
aboard the crew of the Greek
streamer *Artemis*, which had run
aground off Bahia.
1940 Seven round trips Great
Britain-Canada.
Nov: Fitting out as troop transport
commenced at Liverpool, which
lasted until June 1941.
1943 Refitted at Baltimore.
Accommodation for 2,150 troops.
1945 Accommodation ship at
Yalta for the Western participants
in the conference.
1946 Sold to the Ministry of
Transport. Management
continued under Furness.
1950 Renamed *Empire Medway*.
1953 Broken up at Faslane.

1 The Northern Prince, *first of four
sister-ships.*
2 The Eastern Prince, *which served on
the New York-La Plata route.*

1

2

Motorship *Southern Prince*
Furness, Withy & Co, London

1947 *Anna C.*

Builders: Lithgows, Pt Glasgow
Yard no: 816
10,917 GRT; 157.3 × 19.7 m /
516 × 64.6 ft; Burmeister & Wain
diesel, Kincaid; Twin screw;
12,000 BHP; 16.5 kn; Passengers:
102 1st class; Crew: 120.

1929 Mar 12: Launched.
Aug: Completed.
New York-La Plata service.
1940 Troop transport until 1947.
1947 Sold to G. Costa fu Andrea,
Genoa. Renamed *Anna C*. Refit
which lasted until March 1948.
Forepart modernised.
Accommodation for 500
passengers. 11,736 GRT. 159.7 m/
524 ft length overall.

1948 First voyage Genoa-Buenos
Aires.
1952 Re-engined. FIAT diesel,
19,000 BHP. 18, max 20.5 knots.
1960/61 Refit. Passenger
accommodation increased. 202 1st
class, 864 tourist class. 12,030
GRT.
Used mainly for Italy-Central
America service.
1971 Dec 6: Left Genoa for La
Spezia to be broken up.

Motorship *Western Prince*
Furness Withy & Co, London

Builders: Napier & Miller,
Glasgow
Yard no: 267
10,926 GRT; 157.3 × 19.7 m /
516 × 64.6 ft; Burmeister & Wain
diesel, Kincaid; Twin screw;
12,000 BHP; 16.5 kn; Passengers:
102 1st class; Crew: 120.

1929 Jun 20: Launched.
Oct: Completed.
New York-La Plata service.
1940 Dec 14: During a voyage
from New York to Liverpool the
Western Prince was torpedoed by
the German submarine *U 96* 500
nautical miles west of the Orkney
Islands. Crew and passengers
abandoned the ship, which was
sunk 45 minutes later by another
torpedo. 16 dead.

3

3 *In 1948 the* Southern Prince *became
the* Anna C.
4 *The* Anna C. *after her 1961 refit.*
5 *The* Western Prince, *which in 1940
was sunk by a submarine.*

4

5

Lafayette and Champlain

Motorship *Lafayette*
CGT, Le Havre

Builders: Penhoët, St. Nazaire
Yard no: J6
25,178 GRT; 186.8 × 23.6 m /
613 × 77.4 ft; MAN diesel, two
from Penhoët, two from MAN;
Twin screw; 18,000 BHP; 17, max
18.5 kn; Passengers: 583 cabin
class, 388 tourist class, 108 3rd
class; Crew: 472.

1929 May 9: Launched.
1930 Mar: Completed.
May 17: Maiden voyage Le Havre-
New York.
1938 May 4: While being
overhauled at Le Havre the
Lafayette caught fire and was
completely destroyed.
The wreck was sold to be broken
up at Rotterdam.

Turbine steamer *Champlain*
CGT, Le Havre

Builders: Penhoët, St. Nazaire
Yard no: Y6
28,124 GRT; 195.4 × 25.2 m /
641 × 82.7 ft; Geared turbines,
Penhoët; Twin screw; 25,500 SHP;
19, max 21 kn; Passengers: 623
cabin class, 308 tourist class, 122
3rd class; Crew: 575.

1931 Aug 15: Launched.
1932 May: Completed.
Jun 18: Maiden voyage Le Havre-
New York. Cruising.
1940 Jun 17: The *Champlain*
struck a mine near La Pallice and
heeled over in shallow water. 330
dead.
By 1964 the wreck had been
scrapped on the spot.

1 *The* Champlain *in the mid '30s with
a heightened funnel.*
2/3 *The CGT liner* Lafayette, *France's
largest passenger motorship.*
4 *The* Lafayette *on May 5 1938.*

1

2

3

4

SGTM Liner Campana

Turbine steamer *Campana*
SGTM, Marseille

1943 *Rio Jachal*
1946 *Campana*
1955 *Irpinia*

Builders: Swan, Hunter and
Wigham Richardson, Newcastle
Yard no: 1302
10,816 GRT; 160.6 × 20.3 m /
527 × 66.6 ft; Geared turbines,
Parsons; Twin screw; 9,000 SHP;
17, max 17.5 kn; Passengers: 106
1st class, 152 2nd class, 230 3rd
class, 820 steerage.

1929 Jun 11: Launched.
Dec: Completed.
Marseille-Buenos Aires service.
1940 Laid up at Buenos Aires.
1943 Jul 28: Seized by the
Argentine government. Renamed
Rio Jachal. Managed by Flota
Mercante del Estado.

1946 Returned to SGTM.
Renamed *Campana*.
1951 Chartered to Chargeurs
Réunis. Used on Marseille-Far
East service. Passengers: 105 1st
class, 96 2nd class, 56 3rd class.
1955 Jun: Sold to Sicula
Oceanica, Palermo. Renamed
Irpinia. Length overall after refit
and modernisation: 163.5 m /
536 ft; Passengers: 187 1st class,
1,034 tourist class; 12,279 GRT.
Genoa-Central America service.
1962 Refit by Adriatico, Trieste.
New engines, FIAT diesel, 16,000
BHP, 20 knots. Passengers: 209
1st class, 972 tourist class. 13,204
GRT.
Apart from Central America
service, used also for cruising.

1 *The* Campana, *which was completed
in 1929.*
2/3 *The* Irpinia *ex* Campana *in the
'50s (2) and after her 1962 refit (3).*

1

2

3

Delftdijk and Damsterdijk

Motorship *Delftdijk*
Holland-America Line, Rotterdam

1952 *Dongedyk*
1966 *Tung Long*

Builders: Wilton's Schiedam
Yard no: 318
10,220 GRT; 152.4 × 19.7 m /
500 × 64.6 ft; Burmeister & Wain
diesel, H & W; Twin screw; 6,500
BHP; 14.5 kn; Passengers: 50 1st
class; Crew: 54.

1929 Launched.
Oct: Completed.
Hamburg-Rotterdam-Vancouver
service.
1940 North Atlantic service for the
Allies during the war.
1950 Jan 24: The *Delftdijk* struck
a mine in the mouth of the Elbe.
Repaired and rebuilt at Schiedam.
Forepart extended; 161.4 m/
530 ft length overall. New engines:
MAN diesel producing 8,400 BHP
and 16 knots.
1952 Re-entered service after
being renamed *Dongedyk*. 10,942
GRT.
1966 Sold to Taiwan to be broken
up.
Last voyage to Far East as the
Tung Long for the Chung Lien Nav
Co SA, Monrovia.
Sep 12: Arrived at Kaohsiung.

1/2 Holland-America liner Delftdijk
during the '30s (1) and the Dongedyk
ex Delftdijk *after 1952.*

Motorship *Damsterdijk*
Holland-America Line, Rotterdam

1949 *Dalerdyk*
1963 *Presvia*

Builders: Wilton's, Schiedam
Yard no: 322
10,155 GRT; 152.4 × 19.7 m /
500 × 64.6 ft; Burmeister & Wain
diesel, H & W; Twin screw; 6,500
BHP; 14.5 kn; Passengers: 46 1st
class; Crew: 54.

1930 May 17: Launched.
Aug: Completed.
Sep 9: Maiden voyage Rotterdam-
Vancouver.
1940 Aug 7: Seized by the German
Navy. Intended as transport RO 12
for the planned invasion of
England.
1941 Managed by Hamburg-
America Line as a target ship for
the German Air Force and for
submarines. Sometimes used

under the disguise name of
Mülhausen.
1946 Feb 26: The badly damaged
Damsterdijk was returned to
Holland-America Line.
Repaired at Schiedam.
1949 Refit and modernisation.
New Sulzer engines 8,400 BHP,
15.5 knots. Renamed *Dalerdyk*.
1963 Sold to Belvientos Cia Nav,
Panama. Renamed *Presvia*.
Aug: To Japan to be broken up.

3/4 The Damsterdijk *(3) was seized by
the German Navy in 1940 and was to
have been used as transport RO 12 in
the planned invasion of England (4).
5 The* Damsterdijk *was refitted after
the war and re-entered service in 1949
under the new name of* Dalerdyk.

3

Motorship *Johan van Oldenbarnevelt*
Stoomv Mij 'Nederland', Amsterdam

1963 *Lakonia*

Builders: Nederlandsche SB Mij, Amsterdam
Yard no: 194
19.040 GRT; 185.4 × 22.8 m / 608 × 74.8 ft; Sulzer diesel; Twin screw; 14,000 BHP; 17, max 19 kn; Passengers: 366 1st class, 280 2nd class, 64 3rd class, 60 4th class; Crew: 360.

1929 Aug 3: Launched.
1930 Mar 13: Completed.
May: Maiden voyage Amsterdam-Dutch East Indies.
1937 19,429 GRT.
1939 Aug 30: One voyage Amsterdam-New York under charter to Holland-America Line.
1940 Troop transport. Fitted out by Harland & Wolff. Willemstad became her home port for duration of war.
1945 Oct: Released from naval service.
1946 Re-entered Amsterdam-Indonesia service after overhaul.
1950 Sep 2: First voyage Amsterdam-Sydney.
1951 Refitted at Amsterdam for emigrant service to Australia. 19,787 GRT. 1,414 passengers in one class.
1959 Refitted at Amsterdam for round-the-world service. 20,314 GRT. 1,210 passengers in one class.
Apr: First voyage Amsterdam-Sydney-New York-Amsterdam.
1962 Sold to Greek Line, with delivery in 1963.
1963 Overhaul at Genoa with modernisation of passenger accommodation.
Mar 8: Renamed *Lakonia*. From April used for cruising from Southampton to the Canary Islands.
Dec 22: Late evening when 200 nautical miles off Madeira with over 1,000 on board the *Lakonia* caught fire. The blaze spread quickly, claiming 128 lives. The survivors took to the boats.
Dec 24: The Norwegian salvage tug *Herkules* took the burning ship in tow and attempted to reach Gibraltar.
Dec 29: The *Lakonia* heeled over and sank 250 nautical miles west of Gibraltar in position 35°56′ N-10°00′ W.

1-3 *The three stages of the* Johan van Oldenbarnevelt. *Her appearance up to 1959 (1), as a round-the-world liner in 1960 (2) and as the* Lakonia *of the Greek Line.*

1

2

3

Motorship *Marnix van St. Aldegonde*
Stoomv Mij 'Nederland', Amsterdam

Builders: Nederlandsche SB Mij, Amsterdam
Yard no: 195
19,129 GRT; 185.4 × 22.8 m / 608 × 74.8 ft; Sulzer diesel, De Schelde; Twin screw; 14,000 BHP; 17, max 19 kn; Passengers: 366 1st class, 281 2nd class, 64 3rd class, 60 4th class; Crew: 344.

1929 Dec 21: Launched.
1930 Sep 10: Completed.
Oct 7: Maiden voyage Amsterdam-Dutch East Indies.
1937 19,355 GRT.
1939 Laid up at Surabaya.
1940 Troop transport.
1943 Nov 6: While sailing in convoy from Liverpool to North Africa the *Marnix van St. Aldegonde* was torpedoed by German aircraft off the Algerian coast. The 3,000 troops on board were picked up by other ships. The *Marnix van St. Aldegonde* sank the next day during an attempt to tow her into port in position 37°07′ N-6°37′ E.

Motorship *Baloeran*
Rotterdam Lloyd, Rotterdam

1941 *Strassburg*

Builders: Fijenoord NV, Rotterdam
Yard no: 313
16,981 GRT; 174.6 × 21.4 m / 573 × 70.2 ft; Sulzer diesel, De Schelde; Twin screw; 14,000 BHP; 18, max 18.5 kn; Passengers: 236 1st class, 280 2nd class, 70 3rd class, 48 4th class; Crew: 335.

1929 Aug 29: Launched.
1930 Mar 22: Completed.
Apr 15: Maiden voyage Rotterdam-Dutch East Indies.
1937 17,001 GRT.
1940 Seized by the German Navy. Refitted as hospital ship by Wilton-Fijenoord.
1941 Jul 20: Hospital ship *Strassburg*. Managed by Hamburg-America Line.
1943 Sep 1: The *Strassburg* struck a mine north of Ijmuiden. In an attempt to tow her in she had to be beached before reaching harbour because she was so badly holed.
Sep 6: The wreck was abandoned after an unsuccessful salvage

attempt.
Sep 19: Totally destroyed by British MTB's during the night of September 20.

4 *The* Marnix van St. Aldegonde *was torpedoed by German aircraft in 1943.*
5/6 *The* Baloeran, *of Rotterdam Lloyd, became the German hospital ship* Strassburg *in 1941.*

4

Motorship *Dempo*
Rotterdam Lloyd, Rotterdam

Builders: 'De Schelde', Vlissingen
Yard no: 189
16,979 GRT; 174.6 × 21.4 m /
573 × 70.2 ft; Sulzer diesel, De
Schelde; Twin screw; 14,000 BHP;
18, max 18.5 kn; Passengers: 236
1st class, 280 2nd class, 70 3rd
class, 48 4th class; Crew: 335.

1930 Jul 26: Launched.
1931 Feb 21: Completed.
Mar: Maiden voyage Rotterdam-
Dutch East Indies.
1937 17,024 GRT.
1940 The *Dempo* became a troop
transport.
1944 Mar 17: While sailing in
convoy from Naples to North
Africa the *Dempo* was torpedoed
and sunk by the German
submarine *U 371* between Algiers
and Philippeville in position
37°08′ N-5°27′ E.

7/8 *The motorship* Dempo *before the
war (7) and as a troop transport (8).*

7

8

Motorship *Amerika*
East Asiatic Co, Copenhagen

Builders: Burmeister & Wain,
Copenhagen
Yard no: 559
10,110 GRT; 147.6 × 19.0 m /
484 × 62.3 ft; Single screw; 7,600
BHP; 15, max 16.55 kn;
Passengers: 52 in one class.

1929 Aug 22: Launched.
1930 Jan 21: Completed.
Jan 23: Maiden voyage
Copenhagen-Siam. Then on
Copenhagen-west coast of North
America service.
1937 10,218 GRT.
1940 Following the German
occupation of Denmark the
Amerika sailed under the British
flag for the United Baltic Corp,
London.
1943 Apr 22: The *Amerika* was
torpedoed and sunk in the North
Atlantic by the German submarine
U 306, in position 57°30′ N-
42°50′ W. 86 dead.

Motorship *Europa*
East Asiatic Co, Copenhagen

Builders: Burmeister & Wain,
Copenhagen
Yard no: 581
10,224 GRT; 147.6 × 19.0 m /
484 × 62.3 ft; Burmeister & Wain
diesel; Single screw; 8,300 BHP;
15, max 17.2 kn; Passengers: 64 in
one class.

1931 Feb 7: Launched.
May 20: Completed.
May: Maiden voyage Copenhagen-
west coast of North America.
1940 Apr: Came under the British
flag following the German
occupation of Denmark. Managed
by Canadian National Steamships,
Montreal.
1941 May 3: The *Europa* was
burnt out at Liverpool after a
German air raid.
Broken up at New Ferry on the
Mersey.

Motorship *Canada*
East Asiatic Co, Copenhagen

Builders: Nakskov Skibsvaerft
Yard no: 62
11,108 GRT; 150.3 × 19.6 m /
493 × 64.3 ft; Burmeister & Wain
diesel; Single screw; 8,300 BHP;
16, max 17.6 kn; Passengers: 55 in
one class.

1935 May 16: Launched.
Jul 30: Completed.
Aug 7: Maiden voyage
Copenhagen-west coast of North
America.
1939 Nov 3: The *Canada* struck a
mine two nautical miles east of
Holmpton, near Spurn Head, and
sank the following day.

*1-3 Not one of the three motorships
which the East Asiatic Co used
between Copenhagen and the west
coast of North America in the '30s
survived the war. The three
photographs show the* Amerika *(1),*
Europa *(2) and* Canada *(3).*

1

2

3

Newly-built Motorships for Messageries Maritimes

Motorship *Felix Roussel*
Messageries Maritimes, Marseille

1955 *Arosa Sun*

Builders: A et Ch de la Loire, St Nazaire
16,753 GRT; 173.2 × 20.8 m / 568 × 68.2 ft; Sulzer diesel, Cie Const Mecan; Twin screw; 11,000 BHP; 15, max 16 kn; Passengers: 196 1st class, 113 2nd class, 89 3rd class; Crew: 268.

1929 Dec 17: Launched.
1930 Nov: Completed. Marseille-Far East service.
1935 Refitted at La Ciotat. Forepart extended; new Sulzer diesel fitted. 17,083 GRT; 183.0 m /600 ft length overall; 14,700 BHP; 17, max 18.5 knots.
1940 Jul: Seized by the British at Port Said. Managed as a troop transport by Bibby Line. Home port Aden.
1947 Returned to Messageries Maritimes.
1948 Jun 25: Refit and modernisation commenced at Dunkirk, which lasted until 1950. Only one funnel. 17,080 GRT.
1950 Sep 22: First post-war voyage Marseille-Far East.
1955 Apr: Sold to Arosa Line, Panama. Renamed *Arosa Sun*. Refitted at Trieste for North Atlantic service. 20,126 GRT. Passengers: 60 1st class, 890 tourist class.
Aug 20: First voyage Bremerhaven-Quebec.
1958 Dec: Creditors of Arosa Line, which had run into financial difficulties, had the *Arosa Sun* impounded at Bremerhaven.

1959 Apr 10: Arosa Line went bankrupt.
By compulsory auction the ship came into the possession of a Swiss bank which re-offered her for sale.
1960 Sold to Kon Nederlandsche Hoogoven & Staalfabrieken, Ijmuiden.
Sep 27: Arrived at Ijmuiden.
1961 Refit commenced as accommodation ship.
1974 Sold to the Spanish shipbreakers Hierros Ardes.
Mar 28: Arrived at Bilbao.

1-3 *The original square funnels of the* Felix Roussel *were replaced by one oval funnel in 1950.*
4 *The accommodation ship* Arosa Sun *at Ijmuiden.*

1

2

3

4

Motorship *Georges Philippar*
Messageries Maritimes, Marseille

Builders: A et Ch de la Loire, St.
Nazaire
17,539 GRT; 172.7 × 20.8 m /
567 × 68.2 ft; Sulzer diesel, Cie
Const Mecan; Twin screw; 11,600
BHP; 15, max 17 kn; Passengers:
196 1st class, 110 2nd class, 89 3rd
class, 650 steerage; Crew: 260.

1930 Nov 6: Launched.
1931 Completed.
1932 Feb 26: Maiden voyage
Marseille-Far East.
May 16: Returning from her
maiden voyage the *Georges
Philippar* was in the Gulf of Aden
when at 02.00 hrs an electric
rectifier caught fire. Despite
immediate action it was not

possible to bring the fire under
control. The master gave the order
to stop the ship and to start
embarking the 767 people on
board into lifeboats. The survivors
were picked up by three ships
which responded to SOS calls, the
Soviet tanker *Sovetskaia Neft* and
the British cargo vessels
Contractor and *Mahsud*. 54
passengers died in the fire.
May 19: The *Georges Philippar*
sank 145 nautical miles northeast
of Cape Guardafui.

5/6 *While returning from her maiden
voyage the* Georges Philippar (5) *was
destroyed in the Gulf of Aden by a
fierce fire.*

5

Motorship *Aramis*
Messageries Maritimes, Marseille

1942 *Teia Maru*

Builders: F et Ch de la
Méditerranée, La Seyne
Yard no: 1206
17,537 GRT; 172.5 × 21.2 m /
566 × 69.6 ft; Sulzer diesel, Cie
Const Mecan; 11,600 BHP; 15,
max 17 kn; Passengers: 196 1st
class, 110 2nd class, 89 3rd class,
650 steerage; Crew: 260.

1931 Jun 30: Launched.
1932 Aug: Completed.
Oct 21: Maiden voyage Marseille-
Far East.
1935/36 Refitted. New Sulzer
diesel producing 14,700 BHP and
18 knot cruising speed.
1936 Apr 20: First voyage after
refit.
1939 Fitted out at Saigon as
auxiliary cruiser.
1942 Apr: Seized by the Japanese
at Saigon. Taken over as transport
Teia Maru.
1943 Temporarily used as a mercy
ship.
1944 Aug 18: The *Teia Maru* was

torpedoed by the US submarine
Rasher 150 nautical miles west of
Negra Point, Luzon, and sank in
position 18°12′N-120°20′ E.

7 *The* Aramis *in 1932.*
8 *The* Jean Laborde *was used for the
Marseille-Madagascar service.*
9 *The* Jean Laborde *after 1936.*

Motorship *Jean Laborde*
Messageries Maritimes, Marseille

Builders: Constructions Navales,
La Ciotat
11,414 GRT; 149.7 × 18.8 m /
491 × 61.7 ft; Burmeister & Wain
diesel, Schneider; Twin screw;
8,600 BHP; 15, max 16.4 kn;
Passengers: 138 1st class, 92 2nd
class, 76 3rd class, 594 steerage.

1929 Sep 29: Launched.
1931 Jan 24: Completed.
Mar 20: Maiden voyage Marseille-
Madagascar.
1936 Forepart extended. New
Burmeister & Wain diesel from
Schneider & Cie. 11,591 GRT.
157.5 m /517 ft length overall.
9,800 BHP for max 19 knots.
1940 Laid up at Marseille.
1944 Aug: Sunk by the Germans
during their retreat from
Marseille.
1946 Raised.
Apr: Arrived at La Seyne for
repairs. However, the *Jean
Laborde* was so badly damaged
that she was sold to be broken up.

7

Motorship *Maréchal Joffre*
Messageries Maritimes, Marseille

1941 *Rochambeau*
1945 *Maréchal Joffre*

Builders: Constructions Navales,
La Ciotat
Yard no: 156
11,756 GRT; 150.9 × 19.4 m /
495 × 63.6 ft; Burmeister & Wain
diesel, Schneider; Twin screw;
6,800 BHP; 15 kn; Passengers: 138
1st class, 92 2nd class, 76 3rd
class, 592 steerage.

1931 May 14: Launched.
1933 Completed.
Mar: Maiden voyage. Used in
Marseille-Madagascar and Far
East service.
1941 Dec 12: Seized at Manila by
the USA. Fitted out as US Army
transport.
1942 Apr 27: Renamed
Rochambeau.
1945 Mar 17: Released from
service of US Army.

Handed back to Messageries
Maritimes. Renamed *Maréchal
Joffre*.
1950 Mar 30: Arrived at La Ciotat
for refit. Only one funnel.
Passengers: 129 1st class, 130 2nd
class. 11,680 GRT.
1951 Sep: Marseille-Far East
service again.
1960 Jan 15: Arrived at Osaka to
be broken up.

Motorship *Président Doumer*
Messageries Maritimes, Marseille

Builders: Constructions Navales,
La Ciotat
11,898 GRT; 150.0 × 19.5 m /
492 × 64.0 ft; Burmeister & Wain
diesel, Schneider; Twin screw;
10,200 BHP; 18 kn; Passengers:
138 1st class, 95 2nd class, 75 3rd
class, 595 steerage.

1933 Jan 22: Launched.
Completed.
Marseille-Madagascar and
Marseille-Far East service.
1940 First voyage as troop
transport Brest-Norway.
Jul: Seized by the British at Port
Said. Managed by the Bibby Line
for the Ministry of War Transport.
Home port Aden.
1942 Oct 30: The *Président
Doumer* was torpedoed by the
German submarine *U 604*
northeast of Madeira and sank in
position 35°08′ N-16°44′ W. 260
dead.

10

10/11 Maréchal Joffre *as a troop transport (10) and after her 1951 refit (11).*
12 Président Doumer *as an armed transport.*

Empress of Japan and Empress of Britain

Turbine steamer *Empress of Japan*
Canadian Pacific, London

1942 *Empress of Scotland*
1958 *Scotland*
1958 *Hanseatic*

Builders: Fairfield, Glasgow
Yard no: 634
26,032 GRT; 203.1 × 25.5 m /
666 × 83.7 ft; Geared turbines,
Fairfield; Twin screw; 34,000
SHP; 21, max 23 kn; Passengers:
399 1st class, 164 2nd class, 100
3rd class, 510 steerage; Crew: 579.

1929 Dec 17: Launched.
1930 Jun 8: Delivered.
Jun 14: Maiden voyage Liverpool-
Quebec.
Aug 7: First voyage in trans-
Pacific service Vancouver-
Yokohama, for which the ship was
built. The *Empress of Japan* was
the fastest liner on the route.

1939 Nov 26: Troop transport.
1942 Oct 16: Renamed *Empress of Scotland*.
1948 May 3: Released from
transport service.
Refitted at Glasgow and Liverpool
for North Atlantic service. 26,313
GRT. Passengers: 458 1st class,
250 tourist class.
1950 May 5: First voyage
Liverpool-Quebec. From 1952 to
Montreal.
1958 Jan 13: Sold to
Hamburg-Atlantic Line.
Jan 19: Renamed *Scotland* for the
voyage to Hamburg.
Refitted and modernised by
Howaldt Hamburg. 30,030 GRT.
205.2 m /673 ft length overall.
Passengers: 85 1st class, 1,167
tourist class. Renamed *Hanseatic*.
Jul 19: First voyage Hamburg-New
York. Cruising during the winter

months. Managed by Hamburg-
America Line.
1966 Sep 7: The liner was badly
damaged at New York by a fire
which started in the engine room.
The *Hanseatic* was towed to
Hamburg and laid up.
Dec 2: Sold to be broken up to
Eisen & Metall AG, Hamburg.

1/2 *The* Empress of Japan *in the '30s,
(1), and on the North Atlantic route as
the* Empress of Scotland *in the '50s (2).
3 The* Hanseatic, *ex* Empress of
Scotland, *entered service in 1958.*

1

2

3

Turbine steamer *Empress of
Britain*
Canadian Pacific, London

Builders: Brown, Clydebank
Yard no: 530
42,348 GRT; 231.8 × 29.7 m /
760 × 97.4 ft; Geared turbines,
Brown; Quadruple screw; 66,500
SHP; 24, max 25.5 kn; Passengers:
465 1st class, 260 tourist class, 470
3rd class; Crew: 740.

1930 Jun 11: Launched.
1931 Apr 5: Completed.
May 27: Maiden voyage
Southampton-Quebec. Cruising
during the winter months.
1939 Nov 25: Troop transport.
1940 Oct 26: Bound from Canada
to England the *Empress of Britain*
was attacked by a German long
range bomber 70 nautical miles
northwest of Ireland and set on
fire. The passengers and crew took
to the boats and were picked up by
various naval vessels which had
been called to the scene. The
Polish destroyer *Burza* took the
burning liner in tow.
Oct 28: The German submarine
U 32 sank the *Empress of Britain*
with two torpedoes in position
55°16′ N-09°50′ W. 49 dead.

4 *Canadian Pacific's largest passenger
ship, the* Empress of Britain.

Motorship *Cabo San Antonio*
Ybarra y Cia, Seville

Builders: Soc Española de
Construccion Naval, Bilbao
Yard no: 33
12,275 GRT; 152.5 × 19.3 m /
500 × 63.3 ft; MAN diesel; Twin
screw; 7,200 BHP; 15 kn;
Passengers: 200 2nd class, 50 3rd
class.

1930 Jan: Launched.
Apr: Completed.
Entered Genoa-La Plata service.
1939 Dec 29: During a voyage
from Buenos Aires to Genoa the
Cabo San Antonio caught fire
southwest of Dakar and had to be
abandoned. Five dead.
Dec 31: The French destroyer
Cassard shelled and sank the
burnt-out wreck.

Motorship *Cabo San Agustin*
Ybarra y Cia, Seville

Builders: Soc Española de
Construccion Naval, Bilbao
Yard no: 38
11,868 GRT, 152.5 × 19.3 m /
500 × 63.3 ft; MAN diesel; Twin
screw; 9,200 BHP; 16 kn;
Passengers: 12 2nd class, 500 3rd
class; Crew: 112.

1931 May: Launched.
Sep: Completed.
Genoa-La Plata service.
1934 12,589 GRT.
1939 At the end of the Spanish
Civil War, in which she served as
transport for the Republican side,
the *Cabo San Agustin* was lying at
Feodosia, where she was seized by
the Russians.
Renamed *Dnepr*. Placed in service
by the Soviet State Shipping Line
with Odessa as her home port.
1941 Oct 3: During a voyage from
Novorossisk to Odessa, where she
was to evacuate Soviet troops, the
Dnepr was sunk off Anapa by a
torpedo from a German aircraft.
(According to Rohwer/
Hümmelchen, Chronik des
Seekrieges 1939-1945, the *Dnepr*
left Odessa for Sebastopol on
October 5).

Motorship *Cabo Santo Tomé*
Ybarra y Cia, Seville

Builders: Soc Española de
Construccion Naval, Bilbao
Yard no: 39
11,868 GRT; 152.5 × 19.3 m /
500 × 63.3 ft; MAN diesel; Twin
screw; 9,200 BHP; 16 kn;
Passengers; 12 2nd class, 500 3rd
class; Crew: 112.

1931 Launched.
Dec: Completed.
Genoa-La Plata service.
1934 12,589 GRT.
1937 Placed in service as transport
by the Republican troops.
Oct 10: While returning from
Odessa laden with ammunition
and aircraft the *Cabo Santo Tomé*
was attacked off the Algerian coast
by the Spanish Nationalist
gunboats *Dato* and *Canovas*, and
set on fire. One dead. The crew
tried to get the ship to Bône but
were forced to take to the boats as
the fire spread. Shortly afterwards
there was an explosion and the
ship sank.

1 *Ybarra liner* Cabo San Antonio, *the largest ship built in Spain prior to the Second World War.*
2 *The* Cabo San Agustin (*2*) *and* Cabo Santo Tomé *were sister-ships built for the La Plata service.*
3 *Destruction of the* Cabo Santo Tomé.

Turbo-electric vessel *Morro Castle*
Ward Line, New York

Builders: Newport News SB & DD
Co
Yard no: 337
11,520 GRT; 162.0 × 21.4 m /
531 × 70.2 ft; Turbo-electric
propulsion, General Electric Co;
Twin screw; 18,100 SHP; 20, max
21.02 kn; Passengers: 430 1st
class, 100 tourist class; Crew: 220.

1930 Mar 5: Launched.
Aug 8: Completed.
Aug 15: Delivered.
Aug 23: Maiden voyage New York-
Havana.
1934 Sep 8: On a voyage from
Havana to New York the *Morro
Castle* was six nautical miles off
the New Jersey coast near the
seaside resort of Ashbury Park.
There were 555 people on board.
At 02.45 hrs fires were discovered
on the promenade deck and in
room 3 of the forward part of the
ship which had obviously been
smouldering for some time and
which had already got a firm hold.
Despite this threatening situation
the alarm was not given until
03.00 hrs. Attempts were made to
extinguish the outbreaks but the
flames spead very quickly over the
whole ship.

The officers and a large part of the
crew did not appear to be equal to
the situation. Neither did they slow
the ship down, nor authorise the
radio operator to send out a
distress call. At 03.10 hrs an
attempt was eventually made to
bring the ship round oblique to the
wind in order to slow down the
spread of the fire. The *Morro
Castle* was now burning like a
torch. Other ships in the area

made enquiries at land stations
about the fire, which could be seen
for miles around. At last, at 03.23
hrs, the radio operator was
authorised to send out an SOS.
Several ships, as well as the US
Coast Guard, acknowledged the
signal and made for the scene.
Meanwhile, chaos reigned on the
Morro Castle. The flames had
reached the bridge, which was
abandoned. The engine room also
had to be evacuated, and the
engines were stopped at 03.29 hrs.
From the boat deck a total of six
boats were lowered, occupied
mainly by crew members and very
few passengers.
Fortunately, the ships which had
responded to the SOS call reached
the burning liner relatively
quickly. The British *Monarch of
Bermuda* took on 71 survivors, the
American *Andrea F. Luckenbach*
and *City of Savannah* picked up 22
and 65 people respectively. A
further 150 were rescued by fishing
boats and Coast Guard vessels.
The remaining survivors had made
for the coast in the *Morro Castle's*
boats. 133 people died.
The *Tampa* of the US Coast Guard
later tried to tow the *Morro Castle*
but the hawsers broke and the
attempt was abandoned.
At 07.35 hrs the *Morro Castle*
drifted ashore near Ashbury Park,
where she burned for days
afterwards.

Turbo-electric vessel *Oriente*
Ward Line, New York

1941 *Thomas H. Barry*

Builders: Newport News SB & DD
Co
Yard no: 338
11,520 GRT; 162.0 × 21.4 m /
531 × 70.2 ft; Turbo-electric
propulsion, General electric Co;
Twin screw; 18,000 SHP; 20, max
21 kn; Passengers: 430 1st class,
100 tourist class; Crew: 220.

1930 May 15: Launched.
Dec: Completed.
Entered New York-Havana
service.
1941 Jun: Fitted out as troop
transport for US Army.
Oct: Became US Army transport
Thomas H. Barry.
1950 Handed over to US
Department of Commerce.
1957 Broken up.

1 *The fire on the* Morro Castle *remains
one of the most mysterious disasters in
the history of shipping.*
2 *The* Morro Castle's *sister-ship,*
Oriente.

1

2

Turbine steamer *L'Atlantique*
Cie Sudatlantique, Bordeaux

Builders: Penhoët, St Nazaire
Yard no: P6
42,512 GRT; 226.7 × 28.1 m /
744 × 92.1 ft; Geared turbines,
Parsons-Penhoët; Quadruple
screw; 50,000 SHP; 21, max 23.85
kn; Passengers: 414 1st class,
158 2nd class, 584 3rd class; Crew:
663.

1930 Apr 15: Launched.
1931 Aug 18: Completed.
Sep 7: Delivered.
Sep 29: Maiden voyage Bordeaux-
Buenos Aires.
1932 Funnels heightened.
1933 Jan 4: *L'Atlantique* was
sailing without passengers and
with a reduced crew from
Bordeaux to Le Havre, where she
was due to dock. At 03.30 hrs the
ship was 22 nautical miles off the
Channel Island of Guernsey when
a fire broke out in a passenger
cabin on E deck. Four hours later
the fire had spread to such an
extent that the crew had to
abandon ship, taking to the boats
at 08.00 hrs. 19 seamen died in the
fire. The survivors were taken on
board by the *Achilles, Erato, Ford
Castle* and *Ruhr,* which had
answered the distress call.
For two days the burning
L'Atlantique drifted with the tides
and winds in the English Channel.
On January 6 a group of French,
Dutch and German tugs towed her
to Cherbourg. Cie Sudatlantique
abandoned the wreck to the
underwriters. This led to a year-
long legal battle between the
shipping company and the
underwriters, which was eventually
decided in favour of Cie
Sudatlantqiue.
1936 Feb: Having hitherto
remained laid up as *corpus delicti*
at Cherbourg, *L'Atlantique* was
sold to be broken up to Smith &
Houston Ltd, Port Glasgow.

1

2

3

1-3 *In her time the largest passenger ship built for the South Atlantic service,* L'Atlantique *was completely burned out in 1933 after only one year of service.*

KNSM Liner Colombia

Motorship *Colombia*
Royal Netherlands Steamship Co,
Amsterdam

Builders: P. Smit Jr, Rotterdam
Yard no: 454
10,782 GRT; 139.3 × 18.7 m /
457 × 61.3 ft; Werkspoor diesel;
Twin screw; 8,000 BHP; 15, max
16 kn; Passengers: 180 1st class, 66
2nd class, 63 3rd class; Crew: 148.

1930 May 24: Launched.
Nov: Completed.
Nov 28: Maiden voyage
Amsterdam-Central America.
1940 Submarine depot-ship in
Netherlands Navy.
1942 Feb 27: During a voyage
from East London to Simonstown
the *Colombia* was torpedoed and
sunk off the latter port by the
German submarine *U 516*.

1/2 *The* Colombia *was her owner's
largest passenger ship.*

1

2

The Reina del Pacifico

Motorship *Reina del Pacifico*
Pacific Steam Nav Co, Liverpool

Builders: Harland & Wolff, Govan
Yard no: 852
17,707 GRT; 174.9 × 23.2 m /
574 × 76.1 ft; Burmeister & Wain
diesel, H & W; Quadruple screw;
22,000 BHP; 18, max 20.5 kn;
Passengers: 280 1st class, 162 2nd
class, 446 3rd class.

1930 Sep 23: Launched.
1931 Mar: Completed.
Mar 27: Cruising.
Apr 9: Maiden voyage Liverpool-
Valparaiso.
1939 Aug: Troop transport.
1946 Released. To Belfast to be
overhauled and refitted by
Harland & Wolff.
1947 Sep 10: Trials.
Sep 11: Engine room explosion. 28
dead.

In Liverpool-Valparaiso service
again at the end of 1948. 17,872
GRT.
1958 Sold to be broken up at
Newport, Mon.

1 *When she entered service in 1931 the*
Reina del Pacifico *was the largest ship*
on the Europe-Chile route.

1

Motorship *Victoria*
Lloyd Triestino, Trieste

Builders: CR dell' Adriatico,
Trieste
Yard no: 782
13,062 GRT; 164.6 × 21.3 m /
540 × 70.0 ft; Sulzer diesel from
builders; Quadruple screw; 18,660
SHP; 20.5, max 23.26 kn;
Passengers: 239 1st class, 245 2nd
class, 100 3rd class, 82 4th class;
Crew: 254.

1930 Dec 6: Launched.
1931 Jun 21: Delivered.
Jun 27: Maiden voyage Trieste-
Alexandria.
1932 Jan 24: First voyage Genoa-
Bombay.
1936 Oct: Genoa-Shanghai
service.
1938 13,098 GRT.
1940 Troop transport.

1942 Jan 24: During a voyage
from Taranto to Tripoli the
Victoria was attacked by British
torpedo-carrying aircraft in the
Gulf of Sidra and sank in position
33°30′ N-17°40′ E.

1 *The Lloyd Triestino liner* Victoria,
the fastest motorship of her time.

1

Dollar Liners

Turbo-electric vessel *President Hoover*
Dollar Line, San Francisco

Builders: Newport News SB & DD Co
Yard no: 339
21,936 GRT; 199.3 × 24.7 m / 654 × 81.0 ft; Turbo-electric propulsion, General Electric Co; Twin screw; 32,800 SHP; 20, max 22.2 kn; Passengers: 307 1st class, 133 tourist class, 170 3rd class, 378 steerage; Crew: 385.

1930 Dec 9: Launched.
1931 Jun 16: Completed.
Jul 11: Delivered.
Aug 13: Maiden voyage New York-San Francisco-Far East.
1937 Dec 10: While sailing from Kobe to Manila the *President Hoover* struck a reef off the island of Hoishoto at 01.00 hrs. The passengers and crew abandoned the badly damaged ship.
1938 After several unsuccessful attempts to refloat the liner, she was sold in the summer of that year to a Japanese breaker and scrapped on the spot.

Turbo-electric vessel *President Coolidge*
Dollar Line, San Francisco

Builders: Newport News SB & DD Co
Yard no: 340
21,936 GRT; 199.3 × 24.7 m / 654 × 81.0 ft; Turbo-electric propulsion, Westinghouse; Twin screw; 33,000 SHP; 20, max 22 kn; Passengers: 307 1st class, 133 tourist class, 170 3rd class, 380 steerage; Crew: 385.

1931 Feb 21: Launched.
Sep 10: Completed.
Oct 1: Delivered.
Oct 15: Maiden voyage New York-San Francisco-Far East.
1938 The Dollar Line was taken over by the US Government and continued as the American President Line.
1941 Jul 15: First voyage as US Army transport.
1942 Oct 26: Proceeding from Noumea, New Caledonia, and carrying 5,000 men, the *President Coolidge* hit an American mine while approaching Espiritu Santo and began to sink. Thanks to the outstanding discipline on board and the lucky chance that the ship was sinking on an even keel, the vessels that came to the rescue were able to save all but five of the troops and crew.

1/2 *The turbo-electric vessels* President Hoover (*1*) and President Coolidge (*2*) *of the Dollar Line.*

1

2

Turbo-electric vessel *Monarch of Bermuda*
Furness, Withy & Co, Hamilton

1949 *New Australia*
1958 *Arkadia*

Builders: Vickers-Armstrongs, Newcastle
Yard no: 1
22,424 GRT; 176.6 × 23.3 m / 579 × 76.4 ft; Turbines from Fraser & Chalmers, generators and driving motors from General Electric Co; Quadruple screw; 20,000 SHP; 19.5 max 20.75 kn; Passengers: 830 1st class, of which 31 places could be used for 2nd class accommodation as necessary; Crew: 456.

1931 Mar 17: Launched.
Nov 7: Completed.
New York-Hamilton, Bermuda service.
1937 Registered at London.

1939 Nov: Troop transport.
1947 Mar 24: During renovation work at Newcastle for return to passenger service she was almost completely destroyed by fire.
The Ministry of Transport bought the wreck and had it rebuilt by Thornycroft, Southampton, as an emigrant carrier. 20,256 GRT. 1,600 passengers in one class.
1949 Renamed *New Australia*.
1950 Aug 15: First voyage Southampton-Sydney. Managed by Shaw, Savill & Albion.
1958 Jan: Sold to Greek Line.
Feb-May: Refitted and modernised by Blohm & Voss at Hamburg. 20,259 GRT.
Passengers: 150 1st class, 1,150 tourist class. 179.5 m /589 ft length overall. Renamed *Arkadia*.
Registered for Arcadia SS Corp, Andros.
May 22: First voyage

Bremerhaven-Montreal.
1961 Passenger accommodation reconstructed by Blohm & Voss at Hamburg. 50 1st class, 1,337 tourist class. 20,648 GRT.
1966 Dec 18: Arrived at Valencia to be broken up.

1 *The* Monarch of Bermuda, *built as a luxury liner for the New York-Bermuda service.*
2 *The* New Australia *was built out of the wreck of the* Monarch of Bermuda, *which had been destroyed by fire in 1947.*
3/4 *In 1958 the ship was sold to the Greek Line, entering service after her refit as the* Arkadia (*3*). *Picture 4 shows the ship in 1962 after further refits.*

1

2

3

4

Turbo-electric vessel *Queen of Bermuda*
Furness, Withy & Co, Hamilton

Builders: Vickers-Armstrongs, Barrow
Yard no: 681
22,575 GRT; 176.8 × 23.3 m / 580 × 76.4 ft; Turbines from Fraser & Chalmers, generators and driving motors from General Electric Co; Quadruple screw; 20,000 SHP; 19, max 21.07 kn; Passengers: 700 1st class, 31 2nd class; Crew: 410.

1932 Sep 1: Launched.
1933 Feb 14: Completed.
Feb 21: Maiden voyage Liverpool-New York. Then on New York-Bermuda service.
1937 Registered at London.
1939 Oct 28: Armed merchant cruiser in Royal Navy.
1940 Third (dummy) funnel removed.
1943 Troop transport.
1947 Handed back to owners.
1949 Feb: In passenger service again after refit and overhaul. Three funnels again. 22,501 GRT.
1961 Oct: To Harland & Wolff, Belfast, for reconstruction. New single funnel. Projecting stem. 22,552 GRT. 180 m /591 ft length overall.
1962 Feb 23: Trials after refit. Apr 7: In New York-Bermuda service again.
1966 Dec 6: Arrived at Faslane. Broken up by Shipbreaking Industries Ltd.

5-7 *Three photographs of the* Queen of Bermuda: *as a passenger ship about 1935 (5), as an armed merchant cruiser in 1940 (6), and after the 1962 refit (7).*

5

6

7

The Mariposa-Class Matson Liners

Turbine steamer *Mariposa*
Matson Nav Co, Los Angeles

1954 *Homeric*

Builders: Bethlehem SB Corp,
Quincy
Yard no: 1440
18,017 GRT; 192.6 × 24.2 m /
632 × 79.4 ft; Geared turbines,
Bethlehem; Twin screw; 28,450
SHP; 20.5, max 22.84 kn;
Passengers: 475 1st class, 229
cabin class; Crew: 359.

1931 Jul 18: Launched.
Dec 10: Completed.
Dec 14: Delivered.
1932 Feb 2: Maiden voyage San
Francisco-Honolulu-Sydney.
1941 Entered service as US Navy
transport. 18,152 GRT.
1946 Laid up at Alameda.
1953 Sold to Home Lines,
Panama.
Engines overhauled at Alameda by
Todd Shipyards Corp.
1954 Renamed *Homeric*.
Sailed to Trieste for reconstruction
of passenger accommodation by
the Monfalcone shipyard. 147 1st
class, 1,096 tourist class. 18,563
GRT. Length overall 195.5 m /
641 ft.
1955 Jan 24: First voyage Venice-
New York.
May 3: First voyage Southampton-
New York.
1957 Aug 12: First voyage Le
Havre-Montreal, occasionally
Cuxhaven-Montreal.
1963 Oct: Cruising only, from US
ports.

1973 Jul 1: During a cruise the
ship's dining room and kitchens
were badly damaged by a fire 90
nautical miles west of Cape May.
Jul 16: The *Homeric* arrived at
Genoa for repairs. The damage
turned out to be so extensive,
however, that the idea of repair
was given up.
1974 Jan 29: Arrived at
Kaohsiung to be broken up by Nan
Feng Steel Enterprises Co.

1/2 *The* Mariposa (*1*) *became the*
Homeric *in 1954.*

1

2

Turbine steamer *Monterey*
Matson Nav Co, San Francisco

1956 *Matsonia*
1963 *Lurline*
1970 *Britanis*

Builders: Bethlehem SB Corp,
Quincy
Yard no: 1441
18,017 GRT; 192.6 × 24.2 m /
632 × 79.4 ft; Geared turbines,
Bethlehem; Twin screw; 28,800
SHP; 20.5, max 22.26 kn;
Passengers: 472 1st class, 229
cabin class; Crew: 359.

1931 Launched.
1932 Apr 20: Completed.
May 12: Maiden voyage San
Francisco-Honolulu-Sydney.
1941 Dec: US Navy troop
transport.

1946 Laid up at San Francisco.
1952 Sold to the US Government.
Laid up again.
1956 Feb 9: Bought back by the
Matson Line.
Apr: Refit and modernisation
commenced at Newport News
which lasted until May 1957.
Renamed *Matsonia*. 18,655 GRT.
Length overall 195.5 m /
641 ft. 761 1st class passengers.
1957 May 17: First voyage in San
Francisco/Los Angeles-Honolulu
service.
1963 Renamed *Lurline*.
1970 May 27: To Dimitri
Chandris, Piraeus. Registered in
the name of Ajax Nav Corp.
Renamed *Britanis*. Refitted at
Piraeus for 1,655 passengers in one
class. 18,254 GRT.

1971 Feb 21: First voyage in
round-the-world service
Southampton-Sydney-
Southampton.

3/4 *The* Monterey *as a troop transport
during the Second World War (3) and
under her third name,* Lurline, *in the
'60s.*
5 *The* Britanis.

3

4

5

Turbine steamer *Lurline*
Matson Nav Co, San Francisco

1963 *Ellinis*

Builders: Bethlehem SB Corp,
Quincy
Yard no: 1447
18,021 GRT; 192.6 × 24.2 m /
632 × 79.4 ft; Geared turbines,
Bethlehem; Twin screw; 28,500
SHP; 20.5, max over 22 kn;
Passengers: 550 1st class, 250 2nd
class; Crew: 360.

1932 Jul 18: Launched.
Dec: Completed.
1933 Jan 27: Maiden voyage, a
round-the-world cruise.
Then entered San Francisco-
Honolulu service.
1942 Taken over as a troop
transport by the War Shipping
Administration. 18,163 GRT.
1946 Refit and overhaul which
lasted until 1948. 18,564 GRT.
1948 Apr 15: Re-entered San
Francisco/Los Angeles-
Honolulu service.
1963 Sep: Sold to Dimitri
Chandris, Piraeus. Renamed
Ellinis. Registered in the name of
Marfuenza Cia Mar SA.
Refit by Smith's Dock Co at North
Shields, which lasted until
December. 1,668 passengers in one
class. 195.7 m /642 ft length
overall.
Dec 30: First voyage Piraeus-
Sydney.
1964 Entered round-the-world
service Rotterdam-Sydney-
Rotterdam.
1974 Jul 25: Arrived at
Rotterdam, where a damaged
turbine was exchanged for one
from the broken-up sister-ship
Homeric.

*6/7 The Matson Line placed its third
ship, the* Lurline *(6) on the Pacific
service in 1933. In 1963 the ship was
sold to Chandris and after a refit
entered service as the* Ellinis.

6

7

Turbine steamer *Colombie*
CGT, Le Havre

1945 *Aleda E. Lutz*
1946 *Colombie*
1964 *Atlantic*
1964 *Atlantica*

Builders: A et Ch de France,
Dunkirk
Yard no: 144
13,391 GRT; 155.2 × 20.2 m /
509 × 66.3 ft; Geared turbines,
Penhoët; Twin screw; 9,000 SHP;
16, max 17 kn; Passengers: 201 1st
class, 146 2nd class, 144 3rd class:
Crew: 251.

1931 Jul 18: Launched.
Sep: Completed.
Nov 1: Maiden voyage Le Havre-
West Indies. Cruising.
1940 Laid up at Martinique.

1942 Dec: Seized by the USA.
Became a troop transport.
1945 Jan: Refit as hospital ship
commenced, lasting until April.
Renamed *Aleda E. Lutz*.
1946 Apr 11: Handed back to
France. Renamed *Colombie*.
Served until 1948 as hospital ship
in Indo China.
1948 To Vlissingen to be rebuilt
by 'De Schelde'. New single
funnel. Passengers: 192 1st class,
140 cabin class, 246 tourist class.
13,803 GRT.
1950 Nov: Le Havre-West Indies
service again.
1964 Mar: Sold to Typaldos Bros,
Piraeus. Renamed *Atlantic*, and
renamed again *Atlantica* in the
same year.
Venice-Eastern Mediterranean

ports service. Cruising.
1970 Sold to be broken up.
Partially scrapped at Perama.
1974 May: Towed to Barcelona
and broken up there by D.
Descasa.

1 *The original appearance of the*
Colombie, *as she was built for the*
West Indies service.
2/3 *After the war the* Colombie *was*
rebuilt (2) and from 1964 sailed as the
Atlantica *under the Greek flag.*

1

2

3

Rex and Conte di Savoia

Turbine steamer *Rex*
'Italia', Flotta Riunite, Genoa

Builders: Ansaldo, Sestri Ponente
Yard no: 296
51,062 GRT; 268.2 × 29.5 m /
880 × 96.8 ft; Parsons geared
turbines, Ansaldo; Quadruple
screw; 142,000 SHP; 28, max 29
kn; Passengers: 604 1st class, 378
2nd class, 410 tourist class, 866
3rd class; Crew: 756.

1931 Aug 1: Launched for
Navigazione Generale Italiana,
which had originally intended to
name the ship *Guglielmo Marconi*.
In January 1932 the still un-
finished *Rex* became the property
of the new 'Italia' Flotta Riunite.
1932 Sep: Completed.

Sep 27: Maiden voyage Genoa-
New York, which was held up for
three days at Gibraltar where some
engine damage had to be repaired.
1933 Aug: The *Rex* covered the
distance Gibraltar-Ambrose with
an average speed of 28.92 knots,
thereby winning the Blue Riband
for Italy. Until 1935 the *Rex* was
the fastest Atlantic liner.
1940 Laid up at Bari.
Aug 15: Towed to Trieste.
1944 Sep 8: South of Trieste near
Capo d'Istria, the *Rex* was
attacked by British aircraft using
rockets, and caught fire. After
another rocket attack by the Royal
Air Force the *Rex*, which was
burning from end to end, fell over
on her port side and sank in

shallow water.
1947/48 Scrapping operations
commenced on the spot and were
not completed until June 1958.

1/2 The Rex *was the largest Italian
passenger ship and the only Italian
holder of the Blue Riband.*
3 The Rex *in the harbour of Genoa.*

1

2

3

Turbine steamer *Conte di Savoia*
'Italia' Flotta Riunite, Genoa

Builders: CR dell' Adriatico,
Trieste
Yard no: 783
48,502 GRT; 248.3 × 29.3 m /
815 × 96.1 ft; Parsons geared
turbines from builders; Quadruple
screw; 130,000 SHP; 27, max 29.5
kn; Passengers: 500 1st class, 366
2nd class, 412 tourist class, 922
3rd class; Crew: 786.

1931 Oct 28: Launched for Lloyd
Sabaudo. Transferred before
completion to 'Italia' Flotta
Riunite (founded in January 1932).

From 1937 'Italia' SAN.
1932 Sep: Completed.
Oct 14: Final trials.
Nov 30: Maiden voyage
Genoa-New York.
1939 Laid up at Malamocco near
Venice.
1943 Sep 11: The *Conte di Savoia*
was attacked by Allied aircraft,
caught fire and sank in shallow
water.
1945 Oct 16: The wreck was
raised. Reconstruction was
considered, but would have proved
too expensive.
1950 Sold to be broken up at
Monfalcone.

4-6 *Originally ordered by Lloyd
Sabaudo, the* Conte di Savoia *entered
service for 'Italia' in 1932.
In the early planning stages, the names
Dux and* Conte Azzuro *were
considered.*

4

5

6

Turbine steamer *Corfu*
P & O Line, London

1961 *Corfu Maru*

Builders: Stephen, Glasgow
Yard no: 534
14,293 GRT; 164.5 × 21.7 m /
540 × 71.2 ft; Parsons geared
turbines, Stephen; Twin screw;
14,000 SHP; 17.5, max 19.5 kn;
Passengers: 178 1st class, 200 2nd
class.

1931 May 20: Launched.
The name *Chefoo* was originally
intended.
Sep 24: Completed.
Oct 16: Maiden voyage London-
Hong Kong.
1932 May 20: London-Sydney
service for three round trips.
1934 14,170 GRT.
1939 Nov: Armed merchant
cruiser in Royal Navy.
1944 Troop transport.
1947/48 Post-war overhaul and
refit. Only one funnel, white hull.
Passengers: 181 1st class, 213
tourist class. 14,280 GRT.

1949 London-Hong Kong service
again.
1961 Sold to Mitsui Bussan
Kaisha, Osaka to be broken up.
Renamed *Corfu Maru* for the
delivery voyage.
Aug: Arrived at Niihama.

Turbine steamer *Carthage*
P & O Line, London

1961 *Carthage Maru*

Builders: Stephen, Glasgow
Yard no: 535
14,304 GRT; 164.5 × 21.7 m /
540 × 71.2 ft; Parsons geared
turbines, Stephen; Twin screw;
14,000 SHP; 17.5, max 19.5 kn;
Passengers: 175 1st class, 196 2nd
class.

1931 Aug 18: Launched.
The name *Canton* was originally
intended.
Nov 25: Completed.
Entered London-Hong Kong
service.
1934 14,182 GRT.
1940 Jan: Armed merchant
cruiser in Royal Navy.
1943 Troop transport.
1947/48 Post-war overhaul and
refit on the Clyde. Only one
funnel, white hull. Passengers: 181
1st class, 213 tourist class. 14,283
GRT.
1948 London-Hong Kong service
again.
1961 Sold to Mitsui Bussan
Kaisha, Osaka to be broken up.
Renamed *Carthage Maru* for the
delivery voyage.
May: Arrived at Osaka.

1

1 *The sister-ships* Carthage (*1*) *and*
Corfu *were built in 1931 as two-funnel*
steamers.
2/3 *The* Carthage (*2*) *and* Corfu (*3*) *as*
they appeared subsequent to 1948.

2

3

Turbo-electric vessel *Strathnaver*
P & O Line, London

Builders: Vickers-Armstrongs,
Barrow
Yard no: 663
22,547 GRT; 202.4 × 24.4 m /
664 × 80.1 ft; Turbines from
builders, generators and driving
motors from British
Thomson-Houston Co; Twin
screw; 28,000 SHP; 20, max 23 kn;
Passengers: 498 1st class, 668
tourist class; Crew: 487.

1931 Feb 5: Launched.
Sep 2: Completed.
Oct 2: Maiden voyage London-
Sydney.
1939 The *Strathnaver* became a
troop transport.
1948 Nov: Released from
transport service. Overhaul by
Harland & Wolff, Belfast. Only
one funnel. Passengers: 573 1st
class, 496 tourist class. 22,270
GRT. Cruising speed now 17.5
knots.
1950 Jan 5: First post-war voyage
London-Sydney.
1954 Refitted as one-class ship.
1,252 tourist class passengers.
1962 Apr: Arrived at Hong Kong.
Broken up by Shun Fung Iron
Works.

Turbo-electric vessel *Strathaird*
P & O Line, London

Builders: Vickers-Armstrongs,
Barrow
Yard no: 664
22,544 GRT; 202.4 × 24.4 m /
664 × 80.1 ft; Turbines from
builders, generators and driving
motors from British
Thomson-Houston Co; Twin
screw; 28,000 SHP; 20 max 23 kn;
Passengers: 498 1st class, 668
tourist class; Crew: 490.

1931 Jul 18: Launched.
1932 Jan 10: Completed.
Feb 12: Maiden voyage London-
Sydney.
1939 The *Strathaird* became a
troop transport.
1946 Released from transport
service. Only one funnel after refit
and overhaul. Passengers: 573 1st
class, 496 tourist class. 17.5 knots
cruising speed. 22,568 GRT.
1948 Jan: First post-war voyage
London-Sydney.
1954 Refitted as one-class ship.
1,242 tourist class passengers.
1961 Jul 24: Arrived at Shun Fung
Iron Works, Hong Kong, to be
broken up.

4 *When the* Strathnaver *(4) and*
Strathaird *entered service in 1931/32
they were the first P & O Liners to have
white hulls.*
5/6 *When the three-funnel steamers*
Strathnaver *(5) and* Strathaird *(6) were
reconverted for passenger service from
troopships, their appearance was
modernised by the removal in each
case of the first and third funnels.*

4

5

6

Manhattan and Washington

Turbine steamer *Manhattan*
United States Lines, New York

1941 *Wakefield*

Builders: New York SB Co, Camden
Yard no: 405
24,289 GRT; 214.9 × 26.3 m /
705 × 86.3 ft; Parsons geared
turbines from builders: Twin
screw: 36,620 SHP; 20, max 22.7
kn; Passengers: 582 cabin class,
461 tourist class, 196 3rd class,
Crew: 478.

1931 Dec 5: Launched.
1932 Jul 23: Completed.
Jul 27: Delivered.
Aug 10: Maiden voyage New York-
Hamburg.
1939 Dec 30: First voyage New
York-Genoa.
1940 Jun: Atlantic service ceased
because of war in Europe.
Cruising.
Aug 10: First voyage New York-
San Francisco.
1941 Jun: Entered service as US
Navy transport. Renamed
Wakefield.
1942 Sep 3: While sailing in
convoy from Europe to the USA
the *Wakefield* caught fire in the
North Atlantic and the crew had to
abandon her. However, it proved
possible to take the ship in tow and
get her to Halifax.
Sep 18: The US Navy bought the
ship and had her repaired and
fitted out as a troop transport in
the Navy Yard at Boston.
1944 Apr: Re-entered service.
1946 May: Laid up on the Hudson
as reserve ship.
1964 May 27: Sold to be broken
up to Union Metals & Alloys Corp,
New York.
1965 Mar 6: Arrived at Kearny,
NJ to be broken up.

1 *The* Manhattan *during trials. The
liner's funnels were heightened after a
few months of service.*
2 *United States liner* Manhattan *in
1940 with neutrality markings.*

1

2

Turbine steamer *Washington*
United States Lines, New York

1941 *Mount Vernon*
1945 *Washington*

Builders: New York SB Co,
Camden
Yard no: 406
24,289 GRT; 214.9 × 26.3 m /
705 × 86.3 ft; Parsons geared
turbines from builders; Twin
screw; 36,600 SHP; 20, max 22.7
kn; Passengers: 580 cabin class,
400 tourist class, 150 3rd class;
Crew: 475.

1932 Aug 20: Launched.
1933 Apr: Completed.
May 10: Maiden voyage New York-
Hamburg.

1940 Jan 13: First voyage New
York-Genoa.
Jun: North Atlantic service ceased
following Italy's entry into the war.
Cruising in American waters.
Jul 26: First voyage New York-San
Francisco.
1941 Apr 1: First voyage as troop
transport to Manila.
Jun 16: Entered service as troop
transport in US Navy at
Philadelphia. Renamed *Mount
Vernon* (P 22).
1942 Sep 26: Sold to the US
Government. 22,846 GRT.
1945 Renamed *Washington*.
1946 Jan 18: Released as a trooper
and handed over to the US
Maritime Commission. Laid up.

Apr 2: First post-war voyage New
York-Southampton.
1948 Feb: United States Lines
chartered the *Washington,* which
re-entered the New York-Hamburg
service after a refit. 23,626 GRT.
1,106 tourist class passengers.
1949 29,627 GRT.
1951 Oct: Handed back to US
Maritime Commission. Laid up.
1964 Jun 30: Sold to be broken up
to Union Metals & Alloys Corp,
New York.
1965 Jun 28: Arrived at Kearny,
NJ. Broken up by Lipsett Inc.

4

3/4 *The* Washington *against the New York skyline and as the US Navy transport* Mount Vernon.

Oceania and Neptunia

Motorship *Neptunia*
Cosulich Soc Triestina di Nav,
Trieste

Builders: CR dell' Adriatico,
Monfalcone
Yard no: 252
19,475 GRT; 179.7 × 22.3 m /
590 × 73.2 ft; Sulzer diesel from
builders; Twin screw; 19,500 SHP;
19, max 21.83 kn; Passengers: 175
cabin class, 709 3rd class, 648
steerage; Crew: 253.

1931 Dec 27: Launched.
1932 Sep: Completed.
Oct 5: Maiden voyage Trieste-La
Plata.
1937 Jan: The Cosulich Line was
amalgamated with 'Italia' SAN, to
which it had formally belonged
since 1932.
1940 Troop transport.
1941 Sep 18: During a voyage
from Taranto to Tripoli a convoy
consisting of the troop transports
Oceania, Neptunia, Saturnia and
five Italian destroyers was attacked
by British submarines. The

Neptunia was hit by two torpedoes
from the *Upholder* and sank 58
nautical miles off Tripoli. Shortly
afterwards her sister-ship, the
Oceania, was sunk also. 384
people went down out of a total of
7,000 who had been on board the
two sister-ships.

Motorship *Oceania*
Cosulich Soc Triestina di
Navigazione, Trieste

Builders: CR dell' Adriatico,
Monfalcone
Yard no: 253
19,507 GRT; 179.7 × 22.3 m /
590 × 73.2 ft; FIAT diesel;
Quadruple screw; 22,000 BHP; 19,
max 22.1 kn; Passengers: 200
cabin class, 685 3rd class, 500
steerage; Crew: 250.

1932 Sep 29: Launched. Her name
was originally intended as
Eridania.
1933 Jun: Completed.
Jul 8: Maiden cruise in the
Mediterranean.
Sep: Entered Trieste-La Plata
service.
1937 The Cosulich Line was
amalgamated with 'Italia' SAN,
having been a formal member of
Flotta Riunite since 1932.
1941 Sep 18: Together with her
sister-ship *Neptunia* (qv), the
Oceania was in convoy from
Taranto to Tripoli. 60 nautical
miles from the North African port
the ship was hit by a torpedo from
the British submarine *Upholder*
and disabled. Two Italian
destroyers took the liner in tow.
Four hours later the *Oceania* sank
after two more torpedo hits from
the *Upholder*.

1

1-3 The motorships Neptunia (*1/2*)
and Oceania (*3*) *were built for service
to La Plata by the Cosulich Line. In
September 1941 both ships were sunk
on the same day by the British
submarine* Upholder.

2

3

Caribia and Cordillera

Motorship *Caribia*
Hamburg-America Line,
Hamburg

1946 *Ilitch*

Builders: Blohm & Voss,
Hamburg
Yard no: 493
12,049 GRT; 159.8 × 20.1 m /
524 × 65.9 ft; MAN diesel, B & V;
Twin screw; 11,500 BHP; 17 kn;
Passengers: 206 1st class, 103 2nd
class, 100 tourist class; Crew: 198.

1932 Mar 1: Launched.
1933 Feb 4: Completed.
Feb 25: Maiden voyage Hamburg-
West Indies-Central America.
1940 Naval accommodation ship
at Flensburg-Mürwik.
1945 May: British war prize.
Jul 15: Handed over to the USA.
1946 The *Caribia* was awarded to
the Soviet Union and renamed
Ilitch.
Placed on the Kamtschatka-
Vladivostok route.
1973 13,101 GRT after
modernisation (streamlined
funnel).

1 *Hamburg-America Line motorship*
Caribia.
2 *The* Ilitch *ex* Caribia *at New York in
1946. The ship was in Lloyd's Register
as the* Ilitch *until 1970 and since then
as the* Ilyich.

1

2

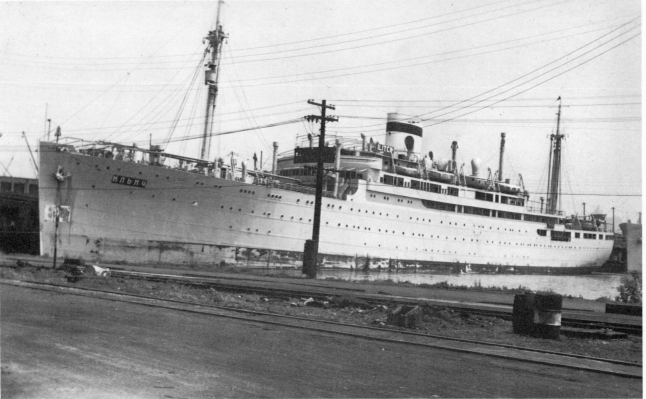

Motorship *Cordillera*
Hamburg-America Line,
Hamburg

1952 *Russ*

Builders: Blohm & Voss,
Hamburg
Yard no: 494
12,055 GRT; 159.8 × 20.1 m /
524 × 65.9 ft; MAN diesel, B & V;
Twin screw; 11,500 BHP; 17 kn;
Passengers: 206 1st class, 103 2nd
class, 110 tourist class; Crew: 195.

1933 Mar 4: Launched.
Jul 29: Completed.
Aug 8: Maiden voyage, a cruise to
the Canary Islands.
Sep: First voyage Hamburg-
West Indies-Central America.
1939 Aug 25: Left Livingstone
without passengers because of the
threat of war.
Sep 10: Took refuge at Murmansk.
1940 Feb 8: The *Cordillera* arrived
at Hamburg from Murmansk.
Naval accommodation ship.
1945 Mar 12: Bombed and sunk
at Swinemünde.
1949 Raised by Soviet salvage
team.
Repaired at Antwerp and
Warnemünde.
1952 Mar: Renamed *Russ* and
placed in service by the Soviet
State Shipping Line. 12,931 GRT.
Used on Vladivostok-
Kamtschatka route.

3/4 The Cordillera *sank at
Swinemünde in 1945. The Russians
placed the ship in service as the* Russ
after salvage and repairs.

3

4

Turbo-electric vessel *Normandie*
CGT, Le Havre

1941 *Lafayette*

Builders: Penhoët, St. Nazaire
Yard no: T6
79,280 GRT; 313.8 × 35.9 m /
1,030 × 117.8 ft; Turbo-electric
machinery from Soc Gén Constr
Electr & Méc Als-Thom;
Quadrupule screw; 165,000 SHP;
29, max 32.2 kn; Passengers: 848
1st class, 670 tourist class, 454
3rd class; Crew: 1,345.

1932 Oct 29: Launched.
Name originally intended to be
Président Paul Doumer.
1935 May 5: Largest ship in the
world until 1940.
May 29: Maiden voyage Le Havre-
New York. On this voyage the
Normandie broke the *Rex's*
record, winning the Blue Riband
with an average speed of 29.98
knots between Bishops Rock and
Ambrose. She broke the record
again on the return journey with an
average of 30.31 knots for the
eastward crossing. In August 1936
the *Normandie* lost the Blue
Riband to the *Queen Mary*, but
won it back again for CGT in July
1937 when she covered the distance
between Bishops Rock and
Ambrose at an average of 30.58
knots. Her average for the same
stretch in an easterly direction in
August 1937 was 31.2 knots. The
Normandie held the Blue Riband
for a year until the *Queen Mary*
broke the record in both directions
in August 1938.
1936 Mar: Measured at 82,799,
then 83,423 GRT after refit.
1939 Aug 28: Laid up at New
York because of the threat of war.

1941 Dec 12: Seized by the US
Maritime Commission.
Dec 24: Taken over by US Navy;
renamed *Lafayette*.
Dec 27: Conversion work to Navy
Transport (AP 53) started.
1942 Feb 9: During welding work
on the promenade deck a fire
started, which, fanned by a strong
wind, soon spread along the upper
decks. Water was pumped by the
ton into the superstructure by the
New York fire brigade, so much so
that the *Lafayette* eventually
became top-heavy. On February 10
the ship heeled over onto her side
at CGT's Hudson Pier.
1943 Aug 7: After extremely
difficult salvage work, in the
course of which the ship's whole
superstructure down to the
promenade deck was scrapped, the
liner was righted.
Sep 13: Raised. Conversion to
aircraft carrier planned.
1945 Oct 11: The *Lafayette,* which
had not been repaired, was struck
from the list of US Navy ships.
1946 Oct 3: Sold by the US
Maritime Commission to be
broken up. The former *Normandie*
was towed to Port Newark and
scrapped by Lipsett Inc.

1/2 The Normandie *entering New
York on her maiden voyage (1) and in
1936 after the rebuilding of the boat
deck aft.*
*3-5 Further photographic studies of
the great* Normandie.
6 The fire on the Normandie *in 1942.*

1

2

3

4

5

6

Motorship *Bloemfontein*
Holland Africa Line, The Hague

Builders: Nederlandsche SB Mij,
Amsterdam
Yard no: 228
10,075 GRT; 148.5 × 19.3 m /
487 × 63.3 ft; Stork diesel; Twin
screw; 8,400 BHP; 15.5, max 16.5
kn; Passengers: 81 1st class, 32
3rd class.

1934 Jun 16: Launched.
Oct 18: Completed.
Oct 27: Maiden voyage in service
Hamburg-Lourenço Marques.
1938 10,081 GRT.
1940 After the German
occupation of the Netherlands the
ship was registered at Batavia for
the duration of the war.
1942 Taken over as transport by
the US War Shipping
Administration.
1946 Apr 10: Returned to Holland
Africa Line.
1948 10,473 GRT after refit.
1959 Aug 8: Arrived at Hong
Kong to be broken up.

Motorship *Jagersfontein*
Holland Africa Line, The Hague

Builders: Nederlandsche SB Mij,
Amsterdam
Yard no: 229
10,077 GRT; 148.5 × 19.3 m /
487 × 63.3 ft; Stork diesel; Twin
screw; 8,400 BHP; 15.5, max 16.5
kn; Passengers: 81 1st class, 32
3rd class.

1934 Jul 21: Launched.
Dec 16: Completed.
Entered Hamburg-Lourenço
Marques service.
1938 10,083 GRT.
1940 Following the German
occupation of the Nederlands the
ship was registered at Batavia for
the duration of the war.
1942 Jun 26: During a voyage
from Galveston to Liverpool the
Jagersfontein was torpedoed by the
German submarine *U 107* 500
nautical miles east of the
Bermudas and sank in position
31°56′N-54°48′W.

1-3 *The sister-ships* Bloemfontein *and*
Jagersfontein (*3*), *which were used on
the Europe-Africa route.*

1

2

3

The Queen Mary

Turbine steamer *Queen Mary*
Cunard White Star Ltd, Liverpool

Builders: Brown, Clydebank
Yard no: 534
80,774 GRT; 310.5 × 36.0 m /
1,019 × 118.1 ft; Parsons geared
turbines, Brown; Quadruple
screw; 200,000 SHP; 29, max 32
kn; Passengers: 776 cabin class,
784 tourist class, 579 3rd class,
Crew: 1,101.

1930 Dec 27: Laid down.
1931 Dec: Building halted
because the Cunard Line was in
financial difficulties.
1934 Apr 3: Building resumed.
Sep 26: Launched.
1936 Apr 15: Completed.
May 27: Maiden voyage
Southampton-New York.
Aug: The *Queen Mary* crossed the
Atlantic between Bishops Rock
and Ambrose at an average speed
of 30.14 knots (west-east 30.63
knots), thus gaining the Blue
Riband from the *Normandie*. In
March and July 1937 the latter won
the trophy back for the eastern and

western crossings respectively. In
August 1938 the *Queen Mary*
covered the Bishops
Rock-Ambrose stretch at 30.99
knots, and did the return journey
at a remarkable 31.69 knots. This
record stood until July 1952.
1937 81,235 GRT.
1939 Sep: Laid up at New York
because of the war.
1940 Mar 1: Troop transport.
Went to Sydney and there fitted
out.
May 5: First voyage as troop
transport.
1942 Oct 2: On a voyage from the
USA to the Clyde the *Queen Mary*
was being escorted by the
British anti-aircraft cruiser
Curacoa. During a false
submarine-alarm 20 nautical miles
northwest of Bloody Foreland
(Ireland) the *Curacoa* came under
the bows of the *Queen Mary*,
which was sailing at full speed.
The cruiser was cut into two by the
liner's stem and sank within a few
minutes. Only 26 of the 364-strong
crew could be rescued.

1946 Sep: Released from
transport service. Overhauled and
passenger accommodation
reinstated by Brown, Clydebank.
1947 July 31: First post-war
voyage in passenger service
Southampton-New York. 81,237
GRT. Passengers: 711 1st class,
707 cabin class, 577 tourist class.
1967 Aug 18: Sold to the city of
Long Beach, California.
Oct 31: Last departure from
Southampton, for Long Beach.
1971 May 10: After considerable
conversion work on the ship's
interior the *Queen Mary* was
opened to the public as a shipping
museum, hotel and convention
centre.

1/2 *The* Queen Mary, *second of the
great superliners of the '30s.*
3 *The last departure of the* Queen
Mary *from Southampton for Long
Beach on October 31 1967.*

1

2

3

The Four Manooras

Motorship *Manoora*
The Adelaide SS Co, Melbourne

1961 *Ambulombo*
1965 *Affan Oceana*
1966 *Ambulombo*

Builders: Stephen, Glasgow
Yard no: 540
10,856 GRT; 146.9 × 20.2 m /
482 × 66.3 ft; Burmeister & Wain
diesel, Kincaid; Twin screw; 8,830
BHP; 16, max 18.5 kn;
Passengers: 260 1st class, 100 2nd
class.

1934 Oct 25: Launched.
1935 Feb 7: Completed.
Apr 11: First voyage in Australian
coastal passenger service between
Sydney and Fremantle.
1939 Dec 12: Armed merchant
cruiser in the Royal Australian
Navy.
1942 Fitted out as landing ship.
1949 Sep 5: First post-war voyage
as passenger ship.
1951 10,899 GRT.
1958 10,952 GRT.
1961 Sold to the Indonesian
Government. Renamed
Ambulombo. Managed by PT
Pelajaran Nasional Indonesia,
Djakarta. Pilgrim service
Indonesia-Jeddah.
1965 Sold to the PT Affan Raya
Line, Djakarta. Renamed *Affan
Oceana*.
1966 Sold to PT Perusahaan
Pelajaran 'Arafat', Djakarta.
Renamed *Ambulombo*. Re-
employed on pilgrim service.
1969 11,111 GRT.
1972 Nov 18: While being towed
by the *Fujisan Maru* from
Djakarta to Kaohsiung, where she
was to be broken up, the
Ambulombo sank off Luzon in
position 18°19′ N-120°34′ E.

Motorship *Duntroon*
Melbourne SS Co, Melbourne

1961 *Tong Hoo*
1966 *Lydia*

Builders: Swan, Hunter &
Wigham Richardson, Newcastle
Yard no: 1460
10,346 GRT; 143.9 × 19.9 m /
472 × 65.3 ft; Burmeister & Wain
diesel, Kincaid; Twin screw; 7,200
BHP; 17, max 19 kn; Passengers:
266 1st class, 107 2nd class; Crew:
151.

1935 Apr 4: Launched.
Jul: Completed.
Coastal passenger service around
Australia.
Oct 12: First voyage Sydney-
Fremantle.
1940 Nov 20: The *Duntroon*
collided with the auxiliary
minesweeper *Goorangai*, which
sank with her entire crew of 24.
1942 Feb: Troop transport.
1950 Aug 25: Back in passenger
service.
1951 10,514 GRT.
1960 Sep 25: Sold to the
Grosvenor Shipping Co, Hong
Kong. Resold to the Kie Hock
Shipping Co, Hong Kong.
1961 Renamed *Tong Hoo* after
refit at Hong Kong. 10,410 GRT.
Entered Hong Kong-Indonesia
service with increased passenger
capacity.
1966 Sold to the Africa Shipping
Co, a subsidary of Kie Hock.
Renamed *Lydia*. Used on India/
Pakistan-East Africa route.
1967 Jul: Laid up at Singapore.
1973 Nov 23: Last voyage, from
Yokosuka to Kaohsiung, where
she was broken up by Hua Eng
Copper & Iron Industrial Co.

1/2 *The* Manoora (*1*) *of the Adelaide
SS Co was sold in 1961 to the
Indonesian Government as the*
Ambulombo (*2*).
3 *The* Duntroon *sailed in the
Australian coastal service until 1960.*

Motorship *Kanimbla*
McIlwraith, McEacharn, Ltd,
Melbourne

1961 *Oriental Queen*

Builders: Harland & Wolff,
Belfast
Yard no: 955
10,985 GRT; 147.6 × 20.2 m /
484 × 66.3 ft; Burmeister & Wain
diesel, H & W; Twin screw; 8,500
BHP; 17 kn; Passengers: 203 1st
class, 250 2nd class; Crew: 160.

1935 Dec 12: Launched.
1936 Apr: Completed. Coastal
passenger service Melbourne-
Cairns or Sydney-Fremantle.
Jun 10: First voyage
Sydney-Adelaide.
1939 Armed merchant cruiser in
the Royal Australian Navy.
1943 Transport and
accommodation ship.
1950 Dec: Returned to her old
routes after naval service. 11,004

GRT. Passengers: 231 1st class,
125 2nd class. When cruising, 371
passengers in one class.
1961 Sold to the Pacific Transport
Co, Panama. Renamed *Oriental
Queen*. Indonesia-Japan service.
1964 Chartered to Toyo Yusen
KK, Tokyo, for Yokohama-
Australia service.
1967 Toyo Yusen KK bought the
Oriental Queen. Australia service
and cruising.

Motorship *Abosso*
Elder Dempster Lines, Liverpool

Builders: Cammell Laird,
Birkenhead
Yard no: 1006
11,330 GRT: 146.5 × 19.9 m /
481 × 65.3 ft; Burmeister & Wain
diesel, Kincaid; Twin screw; 7,200
BHP; 15, max 16 kn; Passengers:
550 1st and 3rd class; Crew: 170.

1935 Jun 19: Launched.
Sep: Completed.
Liverpool-Apapa service.
1942 Oct 29: The *Abosso* was
torpedoed in the North Atlantic by
the German submarine *U 575* and
went down with the entire crew of
168 in position 38°30′ N-
28°50′ W.

4 *The* Duntroon *was sold in 1961 to
Hong Kong as the* Tong Hoo.
5 *Toyo Yusen liner* Oriental Queen *ex*
Kanimbla.
6 *Elder Dempster liner* Abosso.

4

5

6

Turbine steamer *Orion*
Orient Line, London

Builders: Vickers-Armstrongs,
Barrow
Yard no: 697
23,371 GRT; 202.7 × 25.0 m /
665 × 82.0 ft; Parsons geared
turbines from builders; Twin
screw; 24,000 SHP; 20, max 21 kn;
Passengers: 486 1st class, 653
tourist class; Crew: 466.

1934 Dec 7: Launched.
1935 Aug: Completed.
Aug 14: Cruising from
Southampton to the
Mediterranean.
Sept 29: Maiden voyage London-
Brisbane.
1939 Sep: Troop transport.
1946/47 Overhauled and refitted
at Barrow. 23,696 GRT.
Passengers: 546 1st class, 706
tourist class.
Feb 25: First post-war voyage

London-Sydney.
1958 Passenger accommodation:
342 cabin class, 722 tourist class.
1960 May 2: P & O Line and
Orient Line founded a joint
subsidiary company, P & O-Orient
Lines, which employed the ships of
each line.
The *Orion* was then mostly used
as a one-class ship for 1,691
tourists.
1963 May 23: The *Orion* arrived
at Hamburg, where she was used
until September 30 as a hotel at the
Overseas Landing Stage for the
International Gardening
Exhibition.
Oct 1: Having been sold to be
broken up, the ship left Hamburg
for Antwerp. Broken up at Tamise
by J. Boel et fils.

Turbine steamer *Orcades*
Orient Line, London

Builders: Vickers-Armstrongs,
Barrow
Yard no: 712
23,456 GRT; 202.5 × 25.0 m /
664 × 82.0 ft; Parsons geared
turbines from builders; Twin
screw; 24,000 SHP; 20, max 21 kn;
Passengers: 463 1st class, 605
tourist class; Crew: 466.

1936 Dec 1: Launched.
1937 Jul 10: Completed.
Aug 21: Cruising Southampton-
Mediterranean.
Oct 9: Maiden voyage
London-Brisbane.
1939 Oct: Troop transport.
1942 Oct 10: The *Orcades* was
bound from Cape Town to
England with 1,000 troops and
passengers on board when she was
struck by two torpedoes from the
German submarine *U 172* 300
nautical miles west of the Cape of
Good Hope. The passengers and
most of the crew took to the boats.
A remaining 55 volunteers tried to
get the badly damaged ship back
to Cape Town. Although her bow
was lying very deep, the *Orcades*
managed five knots. After a short
time the steering failed. The ship
had to be abandoned, and sank in
position 31°51′ S-14°40′ E.
The survivors were picked up by
the Polish steamer *Narvik*. A total
of 48 people died in the torpedo
explosion and in an accident while
the boats were being lowered.

1

2

3

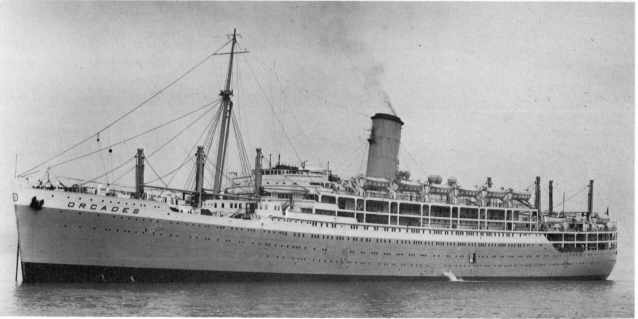

*1/2 Orient Line introduced the corn-
coloured hull for its passenger ships on
the* Orion, *after the colour had been
tested on the* Orama. *Picture 2 shows
the* Orion *as a hotel ship at the
Hamburg Overseas Landing Stage.*
3 *The* Orcades, *sister-ship to the* Orion.

Turbo-electric vessel *Scharnhorst*
North German Lloyd, Bremen

1943 *Shinyo*

Builders: Deschimag AG 'Weser',
Bremen
Yard no: 891
18,184 GRT; 198.7 × 22.6 m /
652 × 74.1 ft; Turbo-electric
machinery from AEG-Weser;
Twin screw; 32,400 SHP; 21, max
23 kn; Passengers: 149 1st class,
144 2nd class; Crew: 281.

1934 Dec 14: Launched.
1935 Apr 30: Completed.
May 3: Maiden voyage. Entered
Hamburg-Far East service.
1939 Sep: Laid up in Japan
following the outbreak of war.
1942 Feb 7: Sold to the Japanese
Navy.
Sep: Conversion to aircraft carrier
commenced by the government
shipyard at Kure.
1943 Dec 15: Commissioned as
escort carrier *Shinyo* in Japanese
Navy.
1944 Nov 17: The *Shinyo* was
torpedoed by the US submarine
Spadefish 140 nautical miles
northeast of Shanghai and sank in
position 33°02′ N-123°33′ E.

Turbine steamer *Gneisenau*
North German Lloyd, Bremen

Builders: Deschimag AG 'Weser',
Bremen
Yard no: 893
18,160 GRT; 198.5 × 22.6 m /
651 × 74.1 ft; Geared turbines,
Weser; Twin screw; 32,400 SHP;
21, max 23 kn; Passengers: 149 1st
class, 144 2nd class; Crew: 281.

1935 May 17: Launched.
Dec 28: Completed.
1936 Jan 3: Maiden voyage. On
Hamburg-Far East service.
1940 Naval accommodation ship.
1942 Conversion to aircraft carrier
planned at the naval yard at
Wilhelmshaven.
1943 May 2: The *Gneisenau*
struck a British aircraft-laid mine
east of Gedser and sank.

Turbo-electric vessel *Potsdam*
Hamburg-America Line,
Hamburg

1945 *Empire Jewel*
1946 *Empire Fowey*
1960 *Safina-E-Hujjaj*

Builders: Blohm & Voss,
Hamburg
Yard no: 497
17,528 GRT; 193.2 × 22.6 m /
634 × 74.1 ft; Turbo-electric
machinery from SSW-B & V;
Twin screw; 32,500 SHP; 21,
max 23 kn; Passengers: 126 1st
class, 160 2nd class, Crew: 262.

1935 Jan 16: Launched.
In the process of the
re-organisation of the German
shipping companies the *Potsdam*
was sold to North German Lloyd,
Bremen.
Jun 27: Trials, followed by delivery
to North German Lloyd on
June 28.
Jul 5: Maiden voyage
Bremerhaven-Far East.
1940 The *Potsdam* became a naval
accommodation ship at Hamburg.
1942 Conversion planned to
aircraft carrier by Blohm & Voss.

Dec 10: Accommodation ship at
Gotenhafen (Gydnia).
1945 Served in the evacuation of
the German eastern territories.
Jun 20: British war prize.
Renamed *Empire Jewel*. Fitted out
as troop transport.
1946 Placed in service by the
Ministry of Transport as *Empire
Fowey*. Managed by P & O Line.
Nov: Laid up on the Firth of Forth
because the Benson high-pressure
boilers were giving trouble.
1947 Mar 11: Rebuilding
commenced by Stephen at
Glasgow, which lasted until 1950.
New boilers and geared turbines.
18,000 SHP, 18 knots. Passengers:
153 1st class, 94 2nd class, 92 3rd
class, 1,297 troops. 19,121 GRT.
1950 Apr: In troop transport
service again after refit.
1958 19,116 GRT.
1960 Mar: Out of service and laid
up.
May: Sold to the Pan-Islamic SS
Co, Karachi. Renamed *Safina-E-
Hujjaj*. Entered pilgrim service
Pakistan-Jeddah.
1964 Besides pilgrim service used
also between Pakistan and Hong
Kong and from 1965 between
Pakistan and East Africa.

*1/2 The North German Lloyd express
steamers* Scharnhorst *and* Gneisenau.
*3 Originally ordered by the Hamburg-
America Line, the* Potsdam *was sold
before completion to North German
Lloyd.*

1

2

3

4

5

4/5 *After the war the* Potsdam *sailed under the British flag as the* Empire Fowey (*4*), *and in 1960 it was sold to Pakistan to become the* Safina-E-Hujjaj.

Polish North Atlantic Liners

Motorship *Pilsudski*
Gdynia-America Line, Gdynia

Builders: CR dell' Adriatico, Monfalcone
Yard no: 1126
14,294 GRT; 160.3 × 21.6 m / 526 × 70.9 ft; Sulzer diesel from builders; Twin screw; 14,000 BHP; 18, max 20.4 kn; Passengers: 355 tourist class, 404 3rd class; Crew: 257.

1934 Dec 19: Launched.
1935 Aug 13: Completed.
Sep 15: Maiden voyage Gdynia-New York.
1939 Refitted in Great Britain as troop transport and placed in service under British control.
Nov 26: During a voyage from Newcastle to Australia the *Pilsudski* struck a mine off the mouth of the Humber and sank. Ten dead.

Motorship *Batory*
Gdynia-America Line, Gdynia

Builders: CR dell' Adriatico, Monfalcone
Yard no: 1127
14,287 GRT; 160.3 × 21.6 m / 526 × 70.9 ft; Sulzer diesel from builders: Twin screw; 14,000 SHP; 18, max 20 kn; Passengers: 370 tourist class, 400 3rd class; Crew: 260.

1935 Jul 3: Launched.
1936 Apr: Completed.
May 18: Maiden voyage Gdynia-New York.
1939 Refitted at Glasgow as troop transport. Placed in service under the British flag by the Ministry of Transport in November. Home port London. Managed by Lamport & Holt.
1946 Handed back to Gdynia-America Line.
Apr: To Antwerp to be refitted for passenger service.
Jul 26: Badly damaged by fire during conversion work.
1947 Apr 1: First post-war voyage as passenger ship from Southampton to New York. On April 30 the ship entered Gdynia for the first time since 1939. Passenger accommodation: 412 1st class, 420 tourist class.
1950 The shipping company changed its name to Polish Ocean Lines.
1951 Apr: At New York the *Batory* was declared an undesirable eastern-block passenger ship and was denied the right to use the port.
Aug 18: First voyage Gdynia-Bombay-Karachi.
1957 Feb: Refit at Bremerhaven with modernisation of passenger accommodation, which lasted until May. Passengers 76 1st class, 740 tourist class.
Aug 26: First voyage Gdynia-Montreal.
1969 Jun: Sold to the Danzig civic administration as a hotel ship.
1971 Sold to be broken up at Hong Kong.
May 11: Arrived at Yau Wing Shipbreaking Co.

1 *Built in 1935, the* Pilsudski *struck a German mine in 1939.*

1

2

3

2/3 *The* Batory *survived the war and sailed in the Gdynia-India-Pakistan service in the '50s, sometimes with a grey hull.*

CGT Mediterranean Express Steamers

Turbine steamer *Ville d'Alger*
CGT, Marseille

1966 *Poseidon*

Builders: Penhoët, St Nazaire
Yard no: Z7
10,172 GRT; 147.6 × 19.3 m /
484 × 63.3 ft; Parsons geared
turbines, Penhoët; Twin screw;
20,000 SHP; 22, max 23.4 kn;
Passengers: 158 1st class, 212 2nd
class, 172 3rd class, 400 steerage;
Crew: 144.

1935 Feb 4: Launched.
Sep 14: Completed.
Sep 20: Cruising St Nazaire-
Algiers-Marseille.
Sep 25: Maiden voyage Marseille-
Tunis-Algiers.
1940 Troop transport.
Laid up at Marseille after French
capitulation.
1943 Jan 6: Seized by the
Germans.
Nov 4: Handed back to CGT. Laid
up at Caronte.
1944 Aug 20: In their retreat the

Germans set fire to the ship and
sank her.
1945 Feb 26: The *Ville d'Alger*
was raised.
Repaired and refitted at Port de
Bouc. Only one funnel.
Passengers: 156 1st class, 422
tourist class, 950 4th class.
1948 Jul 13: First post-war voyage
Marseille-North Africa. 9,890
GRT.
1966 Apr 29: Sold to Typaldos
Bros, Piraeus. Renamed *Poseidon*.
Used on Venice-Piraeus and
Marseille-Haifa routes.
1969 Apr: The *Ville d'Alger*
arrived at La Spezia where she was
broken up.

1 *The* Ville d'Alger *after her
conversion to a single-funnel steamer
in 1948.*

1

Turbine steamer *Ville d'Oran*
CGT, Marseille

1965 *Mount Olympos*

Builders: Constructions Navales,
La Ciotat
Yard no: 158
10,172 GRT; 147.6 × 19.3 m /
484 × 63.3 ft; Parsons geared
turbines, Penhoët; Twin screw;
20,000 SHP; 22, max 23 kn;
Passengers: 160 1st class, 200 2nd
class; 175 3rd class, 400 steerage;
Crew: 144.

1935 Oct 6: Launched.
1936 Sep: Completed. The *Ville
d'Oran* was the property of the
French Government but managed
by CGT.
Oct 17: Maiden voyage Marseille-
Oran.
1939 Fitted out as auxiliary

cruiser following the outbreak of
war. Second funnel removed.
1940 Jun 30: Released from
service while at Dakar.
1941 May: Marseille-Algiers
service until August 1941, then
laid up at Algiers.
1943 Aug: Became a troop
transport for the Allies, managed
by Cunard White Star.
1948 Released from transport
service.
Dec: Refit at La Seyne which
lasted until June 1949. Passenger
accommodation: 188 1st class, 376
tourist class, 671 3rd class.
1949 Jun 22: First post-war voyage
Marseille-Algiers.
1954 Jun 18: CGT bought the
Ville d'Oran from the
Government.
1965 Jun: Sold to Typaldos Bros,

Piraeus. Renamed *Mount
Olympos.* Used on Venice-Piraeus
and Marseille-Haifa routes.
1969 Dec 15: Arrived at Trieste to
be broken up.

2/3 *The second funnel on the* Ville
d'Oran (2) *was removed when the ship
was fitted out as an auxiliary cruiser in
1939. Picture 3 shows her in 1944 as
Allied troop transport.*
4 Mount Olympos *ex* Ville d'Oran.

2

3

4

Bibby Liner Derbyshire

Motorship *Derbyshire*
Bibby Line, Liverpool

Builders: Fairfield, Glasgow
Yard no: 653
11,650 GRT; 153.0 × 20.2 m /
502 × 66.3 ft; Sulzer diesel,
Fairfield; Twin screw; 8,000 BHP;
15 kn; Passengers: 291 1st class;
Crew: 224.

1935 Jun 14: Launched.
Oct: Completed.
Nov 9: Maiden voyage Liverpool-
Rangoon.
1939 Nov: Armed merchant
cruiser.
1942 Feb: Troop transport.
1943 Landing ship, later troop
transport.
1946 Oct: Released from
transport service.
Only two masts after refit and
modernisation. Passengers: 115 1st
class. 10,641 GRT.
1948 Liverpool-Rangoon service
again.
1963 Sold to Hong Kong to be
broken up.
1964 Feb 18: Arrived at Hong
Kong.

1/2 *The* Derbyshire *in the '30s (1) and
subsequent to 1948 (2).*

1

2

Motorship *Dilwara*
British India Line, London

1960 *Kuala Lumpur*

Builders: Barclay, Curle & Co,
Glasgow
Yard no: 654
11,080 GRT; 157.5 × 19.3 m /
517 × 63.2 ft; Doxford diesel from
builders; Twin screw; 6,500 BHP;
14.5, max 16 kn; Passengers: 104
1st class, 100 2nd class, 1,150
troops.

1935 Oct 17: Launched.
1936 Jan: Completed. Purpose-
built for trooping and adaptable
for cruising at inexpensive rates.
1952 12,555 GRT after refit and
modernisation. Passengers: 125 1st
class, 96 2nd class, 104 3rd class,
705 troops.
1960 Sold to the China Navigation
Co, London.
Oct 7: From Southampton to Hong
Kong. Refitted there at the Taikoo
shipyard for pilgrim voyages.
12,598 GRT. 243 1st class
passengers, 1,669 pilgrims. 200
passengers when cruising.
1961 Entered service. Used on
Malaysia-Jeddah and Hong Kong-
Auckland routes. Cruising.
1971 Dec 1: Arrived at
Kaohsiung. Broken up by Tung
Cheng Steel Co.

Motorship *Dunera*
British India Line, London

Builders: Barclay, Curle & Co,
Glasgow
Yard no: 663
11,162 GRT; 157.5 × 19.3 m /
517 × 63.2 ft; Doxford diesel from
builders; Twin screw; 6,500 BHP;
14.5, max 16 kn; Passengers: 104
1st class, 100 2nd class, 1,150
troops.

1937 May 10: Launched.
Aug 23: Completed.
Purpose-built for trooping and
adaptable for cruising.
1951 12,615 GRT after refit.
Passengers: 123 1st class, 96 2nd
class, 100 3rd class, 835 troops.
1961 Refitted by Palmers
Hebburn Co for scholars' cruises.
12,620 GRT. 190 passengers in
cabins, 800 in dormitories.
Apr: First 14 day cruise as a
floating school.
1967 Nov 9: Arrived at Bilbao.
Broken up by Revalorizacion de
Materiales SA.

1 The Dilwara, *prototype for a series of*
motorships built especially for
trooping.
2 *The school-cruise liner* Dunera *in*
1961.

Motorship *Ettrick*
P & O Line, London

Builders: Barclay, Curle & Co,
Glasgow
Yard no: 669
11,279 GRT; 157.5 × 19.3 m /
517 × 63.3 ft; Doxford diesel from
builders; Twin screw; 6,500 BHP;
14.5, max 16 kn; Passengers: 104
1st class, 90 2nd class, 1,150
troops.

1938 Aug 25: Launched.
Dec 12: Completed.
1939 Jan 13: First voyage, cruising
Southampton-West Indies.
1942 Nov 15: During the
homeward voyage from North
Africa to England the *Ettrick* was
torpedoed by the German
submarine *U 155* and sank in
position 36°13′ N-07°54′ W. 24
dead.

Motorship *Devonshire*
Bibby Line, Liverpool

1962 Devonia

Builders: Fairfield, Glasgow
Yard no: 670
11,275 GRT; 157.5 × 19.3 m /
517 × 63.3 ft; Sulzer diesel; Twin
screw; 6,500 BHP; 14.5, max 16
kn; Passengers: 104 1st class, 90
2nd class, 1,150 troops.

1938 Dec 20: Launched.
1939 Jul: Completed.
Aug 11: First voyage as troop
transport.
1953/54 Refitted by Fairfields at
Glasgow. 12,773 GRT.
Passengers: 130 1st class, 96 2nd
class, 99 3rd class, 824 troops.
1954 Feb: Back in service.
1962 Jan: Bought by British India
Line, London, for scholars'

cruises. Renamed *Devonia*.
Refitted for this role by Barclay,
Curle & Co. 190 passengers in
cabins, 830 in dormitories. 12,795
GRT.
1967 Dec 14: Arrived at La Spezia
to be broken up.

3 *P & O Line placed the* Ettrick *in
service in 1938.*
4/5 *Bibby liner* Devonshire *(4) was
sold to British India Line in 1962 and
then made scholars' cruises under the
name* Devonia *(5).*

3

Periodicals
Germanischer Lloyd, Register (Berlin, Hamburg) from 1920
Jane's Fighting Ships (London) from 1938
Lloyd's Register of Shipping (London) from 1920
Weyer's Taschenbuch der Kriegsflotten (Munich) from 1935

Magazines
Die Seekiste (Kiel) 1950-1964
Engineering (London) 1924-1939
International Marine Engineering (New York) 1924-1935
Marine News (Kendal) 1950-1973
Motorship (New York) 1921-1932
Schiffbau (Berlin) 1924-1939
Sea Breezes (Liverpool) 1949-1973
Shipbuilding and Shipping Record (London) 1924-1972
The Belgian Shiplover (Brussels) 1959-1973
The Motor Ship (London) 1924-1939
The Shipbuilder (London and Newcastle) 1924-1937

Books
Anderson, *White Star* (Prescot) 1964
Bonsor, *North Atlantic Seaway* (Prescot) 1955
de Boer, *The Centenary of the Stoomvaart Maatschappij 'Nederland' 1870-1970* (Kendal) 1970
Dictionary of American Naval Fighting Ships (Washington) Vol I-V
Dunn, *Famous Liners of the Past, Belfast Built* (London) 1964
Dunn, *Passenger Liners* (Southampton) 1961
Emmons, *Pacific Liners 1927-1972* (Newton Abbot) 1973
Hocking, *Dictionary of Disasters at Sea during the Age of Steam* (London)
Hümmelchen, *Handelsstörer* (Munich)
Isherwood, *Steamers of the Past* (Liverpool)
Jentschura-Jung-Mickel, *Die japanischen Kriegsschiffe 1869-1945* (Munich) 1970
Kludas, *Die grossen deutschen Passagierschiffe* (Oldenburg and Hamburg) 1971
Maber, *North Star to Southern Cross* (Prescot) 1967
Musk, *Canadian Pacific* (London) 1968
Rohwer, *Die U-Boot-Erfolge der Achsenmächte 1939-1945* (Munich)

Rohwer-Hümmelchen, *Chronik des Seekrieges 1939-1945* (Oldenburg and Hamburg) 1968
Smith, *Passenger Ships of the World* (Boston) 1963
Worker, *The World's Passenger Ships* (London) 1967

Other sources
Archives and publications of shipyards and shipping lines; statements and reports in newspapers.

I should like to register my very sincere thanks for the kind loan of photographs. The pictures in this book were obtained from the following sources:

Marius Bar, Toulon, pages 9/2, 13/9, 64/1, 162/9, 190/1
Baudelaire, Bordeaux, page 9/3
Blohm + Voss AG, Hamburg, pages 38/1, 88/1, 122/1
Bremer Vulkan, Vegesack, pages 44/1, 121/6
Canadian Pacific Steamships Ltd, London, pages 18/1, 102/1, 103/2 & 4, 105/6 & 7, 164/2, 167/4
Cie Générale Transatlantique, Paris, pages 65/2, 124/5, 140/1, 211/1 & 2, 212/3, 233/1
Cunard Steam-Ship Co Ltd, page 95/3
Drüppel, Wilhelmshaven, pages 15/2, 57/1
A. Duncan, Gravesend, pages 13/9, 17/6, 29/5, 35/11, 37/2, 43/2, 45/3, 49/1, 51/6, 55/3, 56/4, 57/5 & 7, 59/9, 62/3, 69/6, 71/3, 81/7, 87/4, 93/2, 97/1, 99/1, 105/8, 109/2, 111/3, 124/4, 133/5 & 6, 139/5, 143/2, 145/1, 161/7, 164/1, 180/1, 183/6 & 7, 185/2, 189/6, 191/3, 197/3, 198/4, 219/1, 221/4, 223/5 & 6, 229/4, 237/1 & 2
L. Dunn, Gravesend, pages 17/6, 25/9, 33/8, 35/12 & 13, 53/9, 61/2, 65/3, 73/3, 85/2, 111/4, 113/6, 195/5, 235/3 & 4
I. Farquhar, Dunedin, page 221/3
S. Gmelin, Cranford, NJ, page 141/3
H. Graf, Hamburg, 29/2, 67/2, 69/5, 75/6, 88/2 & 3, 99/3, 107/2, 123/2, 135/7, 154/1, 163/10 & 11, 172/1, 204/1, 205/3, 207/2, 215/3, 231/2
Hapag-Lloyd AG, Hamburg and Bremen, pages 118/3, 119/4, 125/8, 207/1, 209/3, 227/1 & 2

H. Hartz, Hamburg, pages 21/4, 117/1, 125/6
F.W. Hawks, Horsham, page 63/4
'Italia' SAN, Genoa, pages 47/2, 53/7, 193/2, 195/6
A. Jeske, Hamburg, pages 69/4, 77/9
Dr D. Jung, Berlin, pages 25/8, 27/2, 45/1, 87/5, 88/4, 121/8, 127/10, 147/4, 151/6
R. Kleyn, Voorburg, pages 139/4, 143/3, 157/4, 187/5, 189/7
A. Lagendijk, Enschede, pages 67/1, 91/2, 133/4, 197/2
K.P. Lewis, Bromborough, page 95/4
M. Lindenborn, Capelle ad Ijssel, page 27/1
Lloyd Triestino, Trieste, pages 108/1, 177/1
M. Maass, Hamburg, page 23/6
Mariners Museum, Newport News, pages 99/2, 101/4, 171/1 & 2, 179/1 & 2
H.J. Mayburg, Bremen, pages 37/4, 106/1, 113/5, 131/2 & 3, 191/2
R. Meinecke, Hamburg, page 29/3
Messageries Maritimes, Paris, pages 11/5, 13/6, 157/3
Dr J. Meyer, Rellingen, pages 19/1, 21/3
'Nederland' Stoomv Mij, Amsterdam, pages 41/3, 148/1 & 2, 150/4
Peninsular and Oriental Steam Navigation Co, London, pages 15/3, 28/1, 29/4, 33/9, 128/1, 129/2 & 3, 199/5 & 6, 225/3, 239/1, 240/3
J.F. van Puyvelde, Brussels, pages 7, 71/2, 91/4, 123/3, 141/2 & 4, 157/2, 160/6, 161/8, 213/6
Real Photographs, Broadstairs, pages 43/1, 63/5, 104/5, 187/4
H.J. Reinecke, Hamburg, pages 145/2, 147/5, 181/4, 224/1, 231/3
Rotterdamsche Lloyd, Rotterdam, pages 151/5, 157/3
W.A. Schell, pages 209/4, 230/1
Steamship Historical Society of America, page 186/3
Svenska Amerika Linjen, Gothenburg, page 37/3
United States Lines, Inc, New York, pages 201/1 & 2, 202/3, 203/4
H. v Seggern, Hamburg, pages 23/5, 39/7, 125/7
Wilton-Fyenoord NV, Schiedam, page 146/3
World Ship Society, page 114/8